To Teach

The Journey of a Teacher

SECOND EDITION

William Ayers

FOREWORD BY GLORIA LADSON-BILLINGS

Teachers College, Columbia University
New York and London

Published by Teachers College Press, 1234 Amsterdam Avenue, New York, NY 10027

Library of Congress Cataloging-in-Publication Data

Ayers, William, 1944–
    To teach : the journey of a teacher / William Ayers.—2nd ed.
       p. cm.
    Includes bibliographical references and index.
    ISBN 0-8077-3985-5 (pbk.)
       1. Teaching.   2. Classroom management.   3. Ayers, William, 1944–   I. Title.
    LB1025.3 .A94 2001
    371.102—dc21   00-053634

ISBN 0-8077-3985-5 (paper)

Printed on acid-free paper

Manufactured in the United States of America

08   07   06   05   04   03   02   01   8   7   6   5   4   3   2

To Teach

The Journey of a Teacher

Second Edition

This book is dedicated to my three most persistent teachers:
Zayd Osceola Ayers Dohrn
Malik Cochise Ayers Dohrn
Chesa Jackson Gilbert Boudin

CONTENTS

FOREWORD

Each spring I teach a graduate course entitled "Culturally Relevant Pedagogy." The central question that drives the course is "What does it mean to be a good teacher?" I use that question because I know that we all carry within our own heads visions of what we mean by "good" teaching, and we need to both trouble and problematize our simplistic notions of teaching. One requirement of the course is that students have to choose from one of four teacher narratives to get a sense of how teachers talk about their own practice. From year to year I alter the selections so that students can have the opportunity to choose from some of the more current writing by teachers. However, one book that has remained a constant on the list is Bill Ayers' *To Teach: The Journey of a Teacher*. For this reason, I am pleased to welcome a new edition of this book.

Ayers' book remains a constant because it serves so many purposes of my course wonderfully. It is simultaneously theoretical and practical, triumph and defeat, personal and political, and macroscopic and microscopic. In a word or two, it is the real world of teaching that rarely makes headlines or Hollywood.

My students love this book because in it, Ayers makes himself vulnerable. They learn that very fine lines exist between the mundane and the miraculous, the personal and the political, what works on Monday and what fails miserably on Tuesday. They learn that teaching is such a complex enterprise that the very act of committing one's practice to paper is an act of courage. To lay bare the intimacies of the classroom is an open invitation to critique and attack. Yet Ayers loves teaching so much that he is willing to allow the reader to examine his practice—warts and all.

A favorite aspect of the book is the section of Chapter 1 that outlines some of the pervasive myths about teaching. My graduate students particularly like this one: "Teachers learn to teach in colleges of education," for we all recognize the fallacy that practice is honed in a place of preparation. Lawyers do not learn to practice law in law school. Doctors do not learn to practice medicine in medical school. Lawyers become lawyers in the *practice* of law. Doctors become doctors in the *practice* of medicine. Places of preparation are places where one learns *about* practice and may have an opportunity to participate in practice in a limited and supervised way.

This revised second edition of *To Teach* is important particularly at this time when teaching, schooling, and any attempt to support students' efforts to really learn something of value have fallen under brutal political attack. Ayers raises the substantive question of urban youths—"education for what"—through his description of the ways education can be deployed to create moments of liberation for seemingly despairing young people. Today's education-policy questions about social promotion, standardized testing, and even school uniforms are beside the more fundamental point of what we are preparing students for and how such preparation leads to a more just and equitable society.

To Teach remains one of the few books about teaching that does not disappoint. Bill Ayers takes the reader on a wonderful journey that is filled with intriguing side trips and scenic views. Rather than propose a recipe or formula for teaching success that would invariably lead to failure, Ayers demonstrates an unusual respect for the reader. He asks her to think carefully and critically about the social, ethical, emotional, and political aspects of teaching and to ponder seriously whether she can commit to this noble work of teaching. He refuses to sugar coat the work of a teacher but his work does not, by default, lead us to a place of hopelessness, powerlessness, or despair. He is not the savior or Mr. Chips. Rather, as James Baldwin would say, he is a man who has made a moral choice. The beauty is that he allows us an opportunity to share it.

Gloria Ladson-Billings
University of Wisconsin-Madison

PREFACE

"We love our children," observed the legendary war correspondent Martha Gellhorn in a piece for the *Ladies Home Journal* in early 1967. "We are famous for loving our children, and many foreigners believe that we love them unwisely and too well. We plan, work and dream for our children; we are tirelessly determined to give them the best of life . . . children, we agree, must have security—by which we mean devoted parents, a pleasant, settled home, health, gaiety, education; a climate of hope and peace. Perhaps we are too busy loving our children, to think of children 10,000 miles away, or to understand that [other] people, who do not look or live like us, love their children just as deeply, but with anguish now and heartbreak and fear" (p. 287).

She is writing, of course, about the children of Viet Nam at the time of the American War, but her words resonate as contemporary and urgent. We love our children—famously. And yet in the modern world, our love of children can become dangerously narrowed, constrained, narcissistic, and in the end turn to something other than love, something unintended, something like indifference.

To Teach: The Journey of a Teacher, Second Edition, is a book for teachers and others concerned about the lives of children and youth based on the idea that love of our own and other people's children can be the robust, vivid, and hopeful organizing center of our efforts—it invites teachers and teachers-to-be in particular to rethink the project of teaching from top to bottom, with love at its heart.

This new edition builds on that central idea through several more years of practice and thought and experience, and through regular dialogue with students, teachers, and readers of the original work. The core beliefs and first principles are intact, but more layered perhaps, more applicable to the challenges of today. People are generally drawn to a life in teaching because of a concern for the young, a love of children, a hope to participate in the growth and development of the newer generation. The challenge is to keep love and hope alive in circumstances that are difficult and even deadening, to construct a framework that allows us to see students as three-dimensional and dynamic creatures, and then to continue to deepen and extend that knowledge in the service of more effective teaching.

Most teachers are eager to understand children better, to teach from a solid base of knowing their students. This requires a vision of teaching as intellectual and ethical work, an enterprise that requires a thinking and caring person at the center. Teachers must find ways to sustain those qualities as active and healthy in environments that diminish them, and in situations bent on destruction.

On Valentine's Day 2000 we locked up our two millionth fellow citizen here in the "land of the free." Two million Americans are incarcerated today—1.2 million for nonviolent crimes—more than any other country in the world, six times the number imprisoned in all of Europe combined. One out of three African American boys born today will spend some time in prison in their lifetimes. Black people are six times more likely than whites to be serving time. The price for this embrace of prisons and punishment is steep indeed: the average annual cost of housing an inmate is $20,000; in 1999 we spent $39 billion to cage our fellow citizens.

Along with enthusiastically adopting "discipline and punish" as the last entitlement and the preferred option for every social issue we face, we are retreating as a society from sustained support for education. In the last twenty years, for example, California built 21 prisons and one university, Illinois spent close to $400 million on prison construction and nothing on school construction.

It is this double gesture that may prove disastrous: There is a powerful link between lack of literacy skills and dropping out of school, and the strongest predictor of involvement with the criminal justice system is chronic truancy or leaving of school. If we invest in schools and school improvement, early childhood education and literacy programs, we may reverse this trend; if not, perhaps some time soon we will incarcerate our three millionth neighbor.

As teachers we must fight for the central place of education in building our futures and in developing a robust democracy. Education and democracy are linked: A strong democracy requires a thoughtful, engaged, and active citizenry, and an education that encourages critical thought, reception and resistance, participation and empowerment, will push toward a more vital and inclusive democracy.

The death of hope at an early age is a reality for too many Ameri can youngsters. The cramped choices and strangled life chances for the children of the poor, the "savage inequalities" embodied in social and political decisions allowing the best schools in the world to stand side-by-side with some of the worst, should stir us from apathy, animate our desire to fight injustice, encourage our political responses perhaps.

We all know by now that the state of childhood is not a uniformly happy place, and many of us know the parameters by heart: 22% of American children awake every day in poverty, and black children are three times more likely than white children to be poor. Children are the poorest Americans by far, and 11 million of them have no health insurance. On and on, the hard facts stand in damning contrast to America's vaunted child-centeredness.

Childhood is a time of invention and discovery and surprise, but mostly, childhood is a time of hope. It is a time for the adults in children's lives to dream extravagantly for them, a time for all of us to decide whether our hopes for the future include an investment in the young, and whether our hopes for the young include a robust invitation into the world. All children ought to be supported as they occupy that space of hope, they ought to be allowed to delight in simply being alive as they go forward and stretch themselves into life buoyed by a sense of being unconditionally welcomed. Those of us who work with children must, then, become "specialists in opening small packages," practitioners of the "discipline of hope."

The steady retreat from support for education in America is accompanied by a discourse unimaginable a generation ago: Schools, like any other market, must become profit-driven; if no one wants a kid, he's expendable. We might hold to a different standard: Every child is a multidimensional human being, a person with a heart, a mind, and a soul, with hopes, dreams, aspirations, and capacities that must be embraced if productive growth and learning is to take place. This is the intellectual and ethical heart of our work with children, a standard to rally around and to extend.

Too many schools are characterized by a culture of complaint, passivity, authoritarianism, fatalism, and low expectations. As we work on our teaching projects, we need to counter this culture consciously with our own deepest commitments.

Here is where we can struggle to rescue education from its entanglements and its burdens. For years now I have worked to restructure big failing schools into more intimate communities of learners. Small schools. Bigness in schools was and is deliberate, originally a policy response to the stated needs of the captains of industry, the builders of factories. Big schools tend to be mechanistic and managerial, hierarchical and bureaucratic. Everyone does the same tasks in the same way, like miniaturized factory workers or little soldiers. While all kids are different, in big schools those differences make no difference; youngsters and their teachers are treated as if they are interchangeable parts. Big, comprehensive, competitive schools worked for some and failed for many others. Too many students, alienated from schools, disconnected from education.

Students who drop out say that the main reason they left school is that no adult cared if they stayed. In fact, large, impersonal structures make it terribly difficult to let most students know whether we care if they stay or not. It's hard even to know their names as they stride past us in 50-minute blurs, 30 kids to a class, 150 kids a day. It's impossible to care much, to embrace them fully, to demand much from them. The kids become, then, the crowd, the herd, and much of our teaching bends toward a single goal—to manage the mob. This is the structuring of unethical behavior, the structuring of indifference, the opposite of a calling to the moral dimension.

Small schools are a restructuring strategy aimed pointedly at this disconnection. Smallness is a gesture toward the personal, the particular, the integrated, the supportive. Small schools point toward students at the center of the educational enterprise, every student known well by some caring adult, and every student with the real possibility of belonging to a community of learners. There is, then, a sense of visibility, of significance, of the hope to negotiate here the tricky terrain of identity. The message to children and youth is clear: You are a valuable and valued person here; without you this entire enterprise would flounder and fail.

Small schools point to teaching as intellectual and ethical work, with teachers at the center of classroom practice. Teachers are responsible for the content and the conduct of their work—for curriculum, pedagogy, assessment—and for the school lives of a specific group of students. Teachers are not mindless bureaucrats or soulless clerks. Teachers must become inventors and creators, thinkers and doers.

Our larger goals must be oriented toward the creation of a system that provides a decent, adequate education to all children. There exists now a patchwork of successful and unsuccessful schools. When mapped against socioeconomic status, school success correlates directly with advantage and disadvantage, with race and class. Fighting for change in this critical public arena links to other justice struggles in society, even as it is an immediate effort on behalf of the lives of disadvantaged children here and now.

If we take as our goal the education of all children—or even a gesture in that direction—our system is a failure. It is an unjust system. Our impulse to change must build, then, an opposition to this injustice.

We can bring, of course, knowledge, experience, and thoughtfulness to our efforts to change schools. We can know, for example, the importance of attacking structures of failure and simultaneously the need to disrupt the cultures and standards and expectations of failure. We can work to build capacity at all levels in order to be successful in recultured and restructured schools.

We must bring our commitments with us into our efforts to promote change. School change is an instance of social change, and it is no less complex or demanding than any other. Every change effort occurs in context, and every context bristles with constraints that must be engaged in pursuit of something better, something fairer. Our commitments should include a faith in the ability of ordinary people to shape the solutions to their problems, the importance of rethinking each step as we go, and a willingness to embrace partial measures and small changes that point toward justice.

The collective, ongoing conversation about teaching allows us to glimpse something of the depth of this enterprise, to unearth the intellectual and ethical implications beneath the surface. This conversation is the responsibility of each of us. Talk back, speak up, be heard.

William Ayers

BEGINNING: THE CHALLENGE OF TEACHING

The words teaching *and* teacher *evoke in almost everyone particular memories and images. For some, these memories are dull, even fearful—they include boredom, routine, and worse. For those of us who construct lives in teaching, these images are necessarily changing and growing, and while they are sometimes vivid and concrete, they can as often be characterized by wonder. In either case, images of teaching can fill us with awe, and we can choose to see within them an abiding sense of challenge.*

A life in teaching is a stitched-together affair, a crazy quilt of odd pieces and scrounged materials, equal parts invention and imposition. To make a life in teaching is largely to find your own way, to follow this or that thread, to work until your fingers ache, your mind feels as if it will unravel, and your eyes give out, and to make mistakes and then rework large pieces. It is sometimes tedious and demanding, confusing and uncertain, and yet it is as often creative and dazzling: Surprising splashes of color can suddenly appear at its center; unexpected patterns can emerge and lend the whole affair a sense of grace and purpose and possibility.

I find fragments of my own teaching everywhere, like sections of a large quilt now filling my house, cluttering my mind. I remember Kelyn, a poor, five-year-old African-American child I taught years ago. One day, Kelyn and I, with a half-dozen other kids on a trip from school, were playing the "I Spy" game. "I spy something red and white with the letters S-T-O-P on it," I said. (My choices tend to be the easiest ones, and when too self-consciously geared toward "learning," the most boring as well.) "Stop sign!" cried seven voices in unison.

A big, brown truck pulled up to the stop sign opposite us. Darlene eagerly offered the next challenge: "I spy something brown." Kelyn's eyes lit up and a broad smile crossed his face. He sat up as tall as he could, and with his right hand spread-fingered and flat on his chest and his left hand pulling excitedly on his cheek, he shouted, "Hey! That's me! That's me!"

No one sensed anything peculiar or taboo or funny in Kelyn's response. After all, Darlene had asked for something brown, and Kelyn is brown. But for me there was something more. In that class-room, we had spent a lot of energy on self-respect and affirmation and on exploring differences. Kelyn's father was active in the civil rights movement and his parents were conscious of developing self-esteem in their children. Kelyn was expressing some of that energy, and so he responded with gusto.

Once another child, Duke, asked me to sit with him while he did a portrait in crayon of the two of us. As he drew he talked about what he saw and how he would draw it. "You have yellow, curly hair," he said, "and mine's black and curlier." He didn't draw any noses, and he used two straight lines for our mouths. On another day Duke sud-denly broke out laughing and, pointing at my nose, said, "Your nose is so pointy and straight!" Everyone joined in laughing as I felt it, and guessed that they were right. "And your nose is flat and short," I said. Everyone started describing their own or someone else's nose: Renee's was straight, Mona's short, Cory's like a button—all different, each a new discovery.

Kelyn, Duke, and others were sometimes given to calling one an-other "nappy" or "nigger," and I was painfully aware of hurt and rage. Here, for example is a fragment of writing I found at that time, by eleven-year-old Carolyn Jackson (1966):

> When I ride the train and sit next to a person of the opposite race/
> I feel like a crow in a robin's nest/ And I feel dirty.

Carolyn has a powerful interpretation of what it means to be black in America: to be not wanted; to be "dirty"; to be a "a crow in a robin's nest." This was what I was teaching against, and Kelyn made me feel like we had accomplished a small victory.

I remember another classroom years later and José La Luz, abused and neglected, a posturing thirteen-year-old wise guy whose friends called him "Joey the Light." School failure fit José and followed him around like a shadow. Since he hated school and felt hurt and humiliated there, José made himself a one-man wrecking crew—the path to the principal's office was a deep rut he walked many times.

My struggle was to find something of value in José that we might build on, something he knew how to do, something he cared about or longed for. In March I saw a knot of kids skateboarding over and around some huge drain pipes at a construction site near school, and in the middle of it all, king of the mountain, was José La Luz. I asked José some days later if he could teach a mini-course on skateboarding to the class. He agreed. Soon we were having insignia design contests, subscribing to *Thrasher* magazine, and repairing skateboards on Friday mornings in a shop designed by José in one corner of the classroom. No one lived happily ever after—there was no sudden or perfect turn-around for José—but a moment of possibility, a glimmer of what could be for him, has remained in my mind.

And, finally, I remember a college seminar I taught on curriculum and instruction. The class was based on the notion that learning is a process of active discovery, and that learning depends on concrete experiences and contact with primary sources if it is to be lasting, meaningful, and, most important, if it is to lead to further growth and learning.

In that class we had seen films, read articles, and talked about schools where hands-on learning with children is the norm and not the exception. We had also experimented with discovery learning at our own, adult level. I felt then, as I do now, that it would be virtually impossible to teach in this way if you had never experienced the power of this approach as a learner. One assignment, for example, asked each student to develop an authentic question about the world, a question of some urgency or personal meaning, and then to go out and find the answer to that question by getting close to it, by touching it, and to document the whole process in a variety of ways. Later, students would use the question and the process as a model to develop curriculum with youngsters. While all students—schooled as most of us are in passivity and conformity—had a painful time finding a question ("I don't know what you want us to do." "Would 'the jury system' be an OK question?" "I'm not interested in anything.") some students eventually asked burning questions and were able to pursue sustained inquiries with astonishing results. One student, for example, whose sister was anorexic, investigated anorexia and became involved in an innovative support project for families. Another asked what life was like for the children of alcoholics, and discovered what she had always denied but suspected: that her own mild-mannered, middle-class father was a quiet alcoholic. A hearing-impaired student looked into the reactions of a middle class, residential neighborhood when a live-in facility for mildly disabled adults was established.

What I remember particularly about that seminar was one student—Elaine. Her first attempts at an authentic question had been, "What is the meaning of the Constitution?" and "How are race relations going in Chicago?" Finally she asked, "Where does the woman in the green shoes who I see every day outside Sam Marcy's Restaurant sleep at night?" This question led her beyond a statistical and distanced view of homelessness and into a consciousness-expanding personal journey with Irene, the woman with the green shoes. She discovered a thriving shanty-town within half a mile of the university, a place of community and collectivity as well as of pain and poverty. She traveled to soup kitchens and to church basements, scrounged trash outside restaurants, panhandled at the train station. She uncovered personal histories: Irene's story of the closing of a mental hospital where she was being treated for schizophrenia; John's story of losing his job as a security guard when his firm lost a contract at the airport; Sharon's story of an abusive husband and an ongoing struggle with alcohol. Elaine took pictures and recorded and transcribed interviews. She later developed a dazzling curriculum project filled with energy, experimentation, creativity, and open-endedness. It included an oral history component, a service project at a food pantry, an investigation of government policies and their impact on homeless people, and a weekend with the Mad Housers of Chicago, a group of housing activists who construct simple and livable (but not licensable) structures for the homeless.

———————

Before I stepped into my first classroom as a teacher, I thought teaching was mainly instruction, partly performing, certainly being in the front and at the center of classroom life. Later, with much chaos and some pain, I learned that this is the least of it—teaching includes a more splendorous range of actions. Teaching is instructing, advising, counseling, organizing, assessing, guiding, goading, showing, managing, modeling, coaching, disciplining, prodding, preaching, persuading, proselytizing, listening, interacting, nursing, and inspiring. Teachers must be experts and generalists, psychologists and cops, rabbis and priests, judges and gurus. And that's not all. When we face ourselves, we face memories of our own triumphs and humiliations, of our cowardice and bravery, our breakthroughs and breakdowns, our betrayals as well as our fidelity. When we characterize our work—even partially, even incompletely—straightforward images and one-dimensional definitions dissolve, and teaching becomes elusive, problematic, often impossibly opaque.

One thing becomes clear enough. Teaching as the direct delivery of some preplanned curriculum, teaching as the orderly and scripted conveyance of information, teaching as clerking, is simply a myth. Teaching is much larger and much more alive than that; it contains more pain and conflict, more joy and intelligence, more uncertainty and ambiguity. It requires more judgment and energy and intensity than, on some days, seems humanly possible. Teaching is spectacularly unlimited.

When students describe us, the picture becomes even denser and more layered. Teachers are good and bad, kind and mean, unjust and fair, arbitrary and even-handed, thoughtful and stupid. For our students, we embody the adult world and we are, next to parents, among the strongest representatives of and guides into that world. The hopes and dreams of youth are in our hands; their goals and aspirations are shaped through their encounters with us. Positive memories of teachers are reserved for particular and special people: the teacher who touched your heart, the teacher who understood you or who cared about you as a person, the teacher whose passion for something—music, math, Latin, kites—was infectious and energizing. In any case, teachers are a large presence in the lives of students; we take up a lot of space and we have a powerful impact. This is why I chose teaching: to share my life with young people, to shape and touch the future.

Teachers are asked hundreds, perhaps thousands of times why they choose teaching. The question often means: "Why teach, when you could do something more profitable?" "Why teach, since teaching is beneath your skill and intelligence?" The question can be filled with contempt and cynicism or it can be simply a request for understanding and knowledge: "What is there in teaching to attract and keep you?" Either way, it is a question worth pursuing, for there are good reasons to teach and equally good reasons not to teach. Teaching is, after all, different in character from any other profession or job or occupation, and teaching, like anything else, is not for everyone.

There are many reasons not to teach, and they cannot be easily dismissed, especially by those of us who love teaching. Teachers are badly paid, so badly that it is a national disgrace. We earn on average a quarter of what lawyers are paid, half of what accountants make, less than truck drivers and shipyard workers. Romantic appeals aside, wages and salaries are one reflection of relative social value; a collective, community assessment of worth. There is no other profession that demands so much and receives so little in financial compensation; none in which the state stipulates such extensive and specific educational requirements, for example, and then financially rewards people so sparingly. Slight improvements in pay and benefits in some districts serve only to highlight how out of step we really are when it comes to valuing and rewarding teaching.

Teachers also suffer low status in many communities, in part as a legacy of sexism: Teaching is largely women's work, and it is constantly being deskilled, made into something to be performed mechanically, without much thought or care, covered over with layers of supervision and accountability and bureaucracy, and held in low esteem. Low pay is part of that dynamic. So is the paradox of holding teachers up as paragons of virtue (the traditional pedestal) while constraining real choices and growth.

Teachers often work in difficult situations, under impossible conditions. We are usually isolated from other adults and yet have no privacy and no time for ourselves. We teach youngsters who are compelled by law to attend school, many of whom have no deep motivation or desire to be there. We sometimes work in schools that are large, impersonal, and factory-like; sometimes in schools that resemble war zones. We are subject to the endless and arbitrary demands of bureaucracies and distant state legislatures. Teachers are expected to cover everything without neglecting anything, to teach reading and arithmetic, for example, but also good citizenship, basic values, drug and alcohol awareness, AIDS prevention, dating, mating, and relating, sexuality, how to drive, parenting skills, and whatever else comes up.

The complexity of teaching can be excruciating, and for some that may be a sufficient reason not to teach (for others, it is one of teaching's most compelling allures). Teachers must face a large number of students: thirty or more for typical elementary school teachers, a hundred and fifty for high school teachers. Each youngster comes to us with a specific background, with unique desires, abilities, intentions, and needs. Somehow, we must reach out to each student; we must meet each one. A common experience of teachers is to feel the pain of opportunities missed, potential unrealized, students untouched. Add to this the constancy of change and the press of time, the lack of support and the scarcity of resources, and some of the intensity and difficulty of teaching becomes apparent. It is no wonder that many of us retreat into something certain and solid, something reliable, something we can see and get our hands around—lesson plans, say, or assertive discipline workshops—because we fear burning out altogether.

These are some of the reasons not to teach, and, for me at least, they add up to a compelling case. So, why teach? My own pathway to teaching began long ago in a large, uniquely nurturing family, a place where I experienced the ecstasy of intimacy and the irritation of being known, the power of will and the boundary of freedom, both the safety and the constraints of family living. I was the middle child of five children and I had opportunities to learn as well as opportunities to teach. In my family, I learned to balance self respect with respect for others, assertiveness with compromise, individual choice with group consciousness.

I began teaching in an alternative school in Ann Arbor, Michigan, called the Children's Community. It was a small school with large purposes; a school that, we hoped, would change the world. One of our goals was to provide an outstanding, experience-based education for the young people we taught. Another was to develop a potent model of freedom and racial integration, a model that would have wide impact on other schools and on all of society. We thought of ourselves as an insurgent, experimental counter-institution; one part of a larger movement for social change.

The year was 1965, and I was twenty years old. For many young people, teaching was not only respectable, it was one of the meaningful, relevant things a person could do. Many schools then, as now, were inhumane, lifeless places. But we were crusading teachers. We felt that we could save the schools, create life spaces and islands of compassion for children and, through our work, help create a new social order. We were intent on living lives that did not make a mockery of our values, and teaching seemed a way to live that kind of life. We were hopeful and altruistic and we were on a mission of change.

Today, teaching may not seem so attractive, nor so compelling in quite the same way. Not only are the schools in even worse shape than before, and the problems seemingly more intractable, but there is a narrow, selfish spirit loose in the land. Idealists are "suckers" in the currency of the day, and the notion that schools should be decent, accessible, and responsive places for all children is just more pie-in-the-sky. With a combative social Darwinism setting the pace in our society, and a cynical sense that morality has no place in our public lives, teaching today can seem a fool's errand.

But it is not. Teaching is still a powerful calling for many people, and powerful for the same reasons that it has always been so. There are still young people who need a thoughtful, caring adult in their lives; someone who can nurture and challenge them, who can coach and guide, understand and care about them. There are still injustices and deficiencies in society, in even more desperate need of repair. There are still worlds to change—including specific, individual worlds, one by one—and classrooms can be places of possibility and transformation for youngsters, certainly, but also for teachers. Teaching can still be world-changing work. Crusading teachers are still needed—in fact we are needed now more than ever.

And this, I believe, is finally the reason to teach. People are called to teaching because they love children and youth, or because they love being with them, watching them open up and grow and become more able, more competent, more powerful in the world. They may love what happens to themselves when they are with children, the ways in which they become better, more human, more generous. Or they become teachers because they love the world, or some piece of the world enough that they want to show that love to others. In either case, people teach as an act of construction and reconstruction, and as a gift of oneself to others. I teach in the hope of making the world a better place.

While practically every teacher I have known over many years came to teaching in part with this hope, only a few outstanding teachers are able to carry it fully into a life in teaching. What happens? To begin with, most of us attend colleges or preparation programs that neither acknowledge nor honor our larger and deeper purposes—places that turn our attention to research on teaching or methods of teaching and away from a serious encounter with the reality of teaching, the art and craft of teaching, the morality of teaching, or the ecology of childhood. Our love of children, our idealism, is made to seem quaint in these places. Later, we find ourselves struggling to survive in schools structured in ways that make our purposes seem hopeless and inaccessible. We may have longed for youth-centered communities of shared values and common goals, but mostly we settle for institutions, procedure-centered places characterized by hierarchy, control, and efficiency. We may have imagined the kind of wonderful teachers we could become in an ideal world, but we had no idea of the obstacles that would be scattered along our pathway to teaching.

One common obstacle is the pressure not to teach. Family and friends question the choice to teach, and even experienced teachers advise young people to search somewhere else. One elementary school teacher I know, while in graduate school, worked as an assistant to a prominent education professor who told her repeatedly that she was too bright and too able to be a teacher. She found herself defending her choice against a person she thought would be an obvious ally but was not, and she learned an important lesson: The profession is full of people who don't respect its purposes. If teaching is to become vital and honorable again, it is teachers who will have to make it so. It is the voice of the teacher that must at last be heard.

Another obstacle is the chorus of references to the "real world," as in, "Now this school is the real world." The point is to tell you that you are naive and foolish and that this school is immutable, that it has always been as it is and that it can never be changed. School, in this view, is not an institution of society or history, not something created by people, but rather something outside of history, agency, and choice. Teachers and students alike are supposed to compromise, accommodate, and adjust; to be compliant, conformist, and obedient.

There is a related, even more subtle sapping of your energy and mind as you submit to the structure of schooling. I observed a principal recently welcoming a group of new teachers to his school. Indoctrinating may be a more accurate word. He began by praising these teachers, by admiring their commitment and acknowledging their youthful energy and idealism. They should have known that when anyone praises your youthful idealism, it's time to duck, but instead there were smiles and a sense of worth and pride all around. Then, without changing tone or expression, he began to caution them about the families and the children they would encounter, warning them that they should not expect too much from these youngsters. "Your idealism is wonderful, just what our school needs," he concluded. "But don't blame yourselves if you can't teach these kids to read. It will be enough if you can get them to listen."

All the praise of youth and admiration of idealism turns out to be a cover for cynicism. These teachers are being told to accept something that is really unacceptable, to "grow up," to lower their expectations for learners. It's true that no one is wise before innocent, competent before clumsy. It is also true that teachers need to grow in experience, skill, and judgment. But that growth does not need to be based on narrowing goals, aspirations, and ideals, as this principal would have it. It is true that teaching is the kind of activity that develops and flowers over time, that there is no way to be an experienced teacher without first being a new teacher. But that development can be constructed on the basis of high ideals, hope, realism, and compassion for others. Teachers do, indeed, need to be forgiving of their own inevitable shortcomings, but always in the context of being critical and demanding of themselves as well.

Finally, a major obstacle on the pathway to teaching is the notion that teaching is essentially technical, that it is easily learned, simply assessed, and quickly remediated. Students of teaching spend an inordinate amount of time learning how to make lesson plans (an astonishingly simple, entirely overblown, and not very useful skill) or reading the research on classroom management. We are encouraged to attend to the voice of the supervisor and the administrator, the academic and the researcher, and not to the more immediate and important voices of children and youth, their parents and community. This is, perhaps, the most difficult obstacle to overcome, and resistance and reconciliation are major themes in the act of effective teaching.

———————

I know that I celebrate a kind of teaching that is exceedingly rare. I know that becoming an outstanding teacher is an heroic quest: Like Odysseus one must navigate turbulent and troubled waters, overcome a seemingly endless sea of obstacles, and face danger and challenge (often alone) on the way toward an uncertain reward. Teaching is not for the weak or the faint-hearted; courage and imagination are needed to move from myth to reality.

Teaching is entombed in myth—there are literally thousands of tiny ones clinging like barnacles to teaching, while others perch on it like giant, fire-breathing creatures. These myths are available in every film about teaching, in all the popular literature, and in the common sense passed across the generations. Here is a sample:

MYTH 1

Good Classroom Management is an Essential First Step Toward Becoming a Good Teacher

This myth is central to the everyday lore of teaching. It is the old "don't-smile-until-Christmas" wisdom. Some teachers say, "I get tough in September to gain their respect, and then I can ease up without losing control." Others say, "I play 'bad cop' first so they know who's boss, and then I can afford to be 'good cop.'" Others describe teaching as trench warfare, and claim that control of the trenches is a primary goal.

There is a sleight-of-hand involved here, for it is true that an out-of-control classroom is dysfunctional for everyone. But what makes this a myth is (1) its linearity—the assumption that classroom manage ment precedes teaching in time and (2) its insularity—the notion that classroom management can sensibly be understood as an event separated from the whole of teaching. The classroom management myth represents, in a sense, the triumph of narrow behaviorism and manipulation over teaching as a moral craft and an intellectual enterprise.

The ability to work productively with a large group of students is a skill that only comes with experience. The development of that skill is not aided by focusing on techniques from the pantheon of classroom management: "positive reinforcement," "anticipatory set," "wait time," and all the rest. Those simply turn a teacher's attention in the wrong direction. Nor is it useful to assume that once in control, teaching can begin. There are a lot of quiet, passive classrooms where not much learning is taking place, and others where children's hearts, souls, and minds are being silently destroyed in the name of good management.

Working well with a group of youngsters is something learned in practice. And it is best learned not as a set of techniques to shape behavior without regard to persons or values, but while attempting to accomplish larger goals and purposes. This means focusing on three essentials: youngsters (Are they active? Are they pursuing questions and concerns of importance to them and us?); the environment (Is it appropriate? Does it offer sufficient challenge? Are there multiple opportunities to succeed?); and curriculum (Is it engaging? Does it connect the known to the unknown?). While this will not yield instant "results," it will allow for the emergence of more authentic and productive teachers and teaching relationships, and questions of group coherence and standards of behavior can then be worked out in context.

MYTH 2

Teachers Learn to Teach in Colleges of Education

This myth floats pervasively (if uneasily) on the surface of society as a whole, but teachers don't believe it for a minute. Teachers know that they learned to teach on the job (and unfortunately, some of what is learned on the job is never subjected to serious scrutiny), and that their journey through teacher education was painfully dull, occasionally malevolent, and mostly beside the point. Some teachers believe that a few college courses could have been useful if they had been offered during the first years of actual classroom experience, instead of being dished out as "truth" disconnected from the messy reality of schools.

When teacher education programs structure the separation of theory and practice, this message alone is enough to degrade teaching. When we imply that teaching is quickly learned and easily fixed (like learning the fox trot); that it is based on methods and techniques or on little formulas; that it is generic, in the sense that learning to teach in Hannibal equips a teacher for teaching in Harlem—then teaching can be killed off entirely.

Teaching is an eminently practical activity, best learned in the exercise of it and in the thoughtful reflection that must accompany that. This reflection should be structured into the teaching day, and should be conducted with peers, and with more experienced people who can act as coaches or guides, and can direct a probingly critical eye at every detail of school life. The complexity of real teaching can then be grasped, and the intellectual and ethical heart of teaching can be kept in its center.

MYTH 3

Good Teachers Are Always Fun

Fun is distracting, amusing, diverting. Clowns are fun. Jokes can be fun. Learning can be engaging, engrossing, amazing, disorienting, involving, and often deeply pleasurable. If it's delightful, joyful, or festive, even better. But it doesn't need to be fun. Imagine falling in love, connecting with your loved one in intimate embrace, making love, and finding yourself for the first time really known and understood, transported and transformed. If, as you looked deeply into those beloved eyes, your lover said, "That was fun," it would utterly destroy the moment. Good teachers are not always fun; good teachers should aim always for authentic engagement with students.

MYTH 4

Good Teachers Always Know the Materials

This is tricky. On the one hand, teachers need to know a lot, and good teachers are always reading, wondering, exploring—always expanding their interests and their knowledge. Who would argue for knowing less? On the other hand, since the universe is expanding and knowledge is infinite there is simply no way for any teacher to know everything. The game some teachers play of trying to stay one step ahead in the text in order to teach the material is ludicrous. That game assumes that knowledge is finite and that teaching is a matter of conveying the same limited stuff to students, who are themselves beneath respect, incapable of thinking outside the informational realm of "one step forward at a time."

Many fine teachers plunge into the unknown alongside their students, simultaneously enacting productive approaches to learning and demonstrating desirable dispositions of mind, like courage and curiosity. A unit on machines in elementary school might involve bringing in broken household appliances and working together to understand how they function. A unit on Asian immigration in high school might involve a collective search through newspaper archives or interviews in the community. Learning with students can be a powerful approach to teaching. Good teachers often teach precisely so that they can learn.

MYTH 5

Good Teachers Begin With the Curriculum They Are Given and Find Clever Ways to Enhance It

Good teachers begin with high hopes and deep expectations for learners and struggle to meet those expectation in every instance. Too often the question is, "Is it practical?" when the question ought to be, "Is it passionate?" The given curriculum can be a guide or an obstacle, a framework or a hindrance, a resource or a barrier. The point is to get the job done, and sometimes that means starting elsewhere and circling back to the official curriculum simply to satisfy administrators.

For example, my brother teaches English at Berkeley High School. In a class in which he was required to teach Shakespeare's *The Tempest*, he decided to surround that reading, as well, with Bertold Brecht, William Golding, Kenzaburo Oe, and much more. The syllabus he wrote began in an interestingly original place:

"Do you ever wonder why the world is so messed up? Do you ever think to yourself what kind of society you would create if you could just start over? Plenty of people have tried just that, either in writing stories or in actually remaking governments. This year we are going to spend a long time considering our society and many alternatives. We will always be looking to answer the question: What are the characteristics of a just society? We will begin with *The Tempest* . . . a play about a strange magical land. . . . On this island an exile from Milan has created his world, a regime of secret followers and spirits. Would you like to live there? Of course, everything depends on your point of view: the world looks different through the eyes of the master and of the slave. In Brecht's poem 'A Worker Reads History' he asks, Who built the pyramids? Not the Pharoah; who did the actual work?"

And so on.

MYTH 6

Good Teachers Are Good Performers

Sometimes. But just as often, good teachers are not charismatic and are not exhibitionists. Certainly they are not "center stage," because that place is reserved for students.

When I taught preschool, much of my work was behind the scenes, quiet, unobtrusive. One year, a student teacher paid me a high compliment: "For two months, I didn't think you were doing anything. Your teaching was indirect, seamless, and subtle, and the kids' work was all that I could see."

This myth of teachers as performers strips teaching of much of its depth and texture and is linked to the idea that teaching is telling, that teaching is delivering lessons or dispensing knowledge. This is a tiny part of teaching, and yet in myth it is elevated to the whole of it.

MYTH 7

Good Teachers Treat all Students Alike

It is important for teachers to be fair, to be thoughtful, to be caring in relation to all students. If all students were the same then a good teacher would treat them all the same. But here is Sonia with an explosive anger that can take over the room, and she needs more; here is James, whose mother died recently, and he needs more; here is Angel, who cannot speak English, and he needs more. Needs shift and change. When I was a new teacher and Kevin showed up one day without lunch money, I gave him the necessary 50 cents; several colleagues encouraged me to let him go hungry or I'd "be buying every kid's lunch every day." It never happened.

In a family, the nighttime fears of one child might take considerable focus and energy for a time, and then the struggle of another child to read takes over. Helping the two children in kindergarten who are having difficulty separating from their mothers assures all children that this is a safe and friendly place. Good teachers spend time and energy where they must, and expect that positive results will spread laterally among the group.

MYTH 8

Students Today Are Different From Ever Before

Every generation of adults tells of a golden age of teaching or parenting when youngsters were well-behaved and capable. This misty-eyed view is typically a highly edited version of their own youth. Some teachers claim to have been outstanding early in their careers, but now assert: "I can't teach these kids." Today, the justifications for this are put in terms of "cocaine babies" and "households headed by women," where once it was the "culture of poverty" and "cultural deprivation," and before that, "immigrants who didn't care about their children."

The fact is that kids come to school with a range of difficult backgrounds and troubling experiences. They come from families, each of which has strengths and weaknesses. Teachers, as always, must resist the idea that there is some ideal child with whom they would be brilliant; they must reject the notion that a child's success is determined by family background or social circumstance; they must respond to the real children coming through the door and find ways to teach them. That has always been a complex and difficult goal, and it will always be so.

MYTH 9

Good Teaching Can Be Measured by How Well Students Do on Tests

Besides the many problems related to standardized testing, there are also problems that revolve around the connection of teaching to learning. Learning is not linear; it does not occur as a straight line, gradually inclined, formally and incrementally constructed. Learning is dynamic and explosive and a lot of it is informal; much of it builds up over time and connects suddenly. This means that teachers have an awesome responsibility, as we shall see, to keep their teaching robust and energetic, for learning is irreducible.

MYTH 10

A Good Teacher Knows What's Going On in the Classroom

Teachers sometimes assume that there is one true story of classroom life, and then thirty misinterpretations. In reality, teachers know *one* story of what's going on, but not the *only* story nor even the "true story." True stories are multitudinous because there are thirty-some true stories. Kids are active interpreters of classroom reality and their interpretations are only sometimes synonymous with their teacher's interpretations. Classrooms are yeasty places, where an entire group comes together and creates a distinctive and dynamic culture; sometimes things bubble and rise; sometimes they are punched down or killed off.

MYTH 11

All Children Are Above Average

There is a pervasive "myth of third grade," as in, "He's reading at the third grade level." It's as if there is an "ideal" third grader somewhere on Mt. Olympus, and everyone else is just a shadow or a pretender. This explains why every fourth-grade teacher is angry at every third-grade teacher, every high school teacher is unhappy with every elementary teacher, and college teachers are miserable with the whole lot—the kids didn't come "ready." The truth is third-graders are various, and the teacher's job is to teach to that variety, that diversity.

MYTH 12

Kids Today Are Worse Than Ever Before

"The children now love luxury. They have bad manners, contempt for authority, they show disrespect for adults, and love to talk rather than work or exercise. They no longer rise when adults enter the room. They contradict their parents, chatter in front of company, gobble down food at the table, and intimidate their teachers."

This version of the myth was written by Socrates about 2,400 years ago. Shakespeare added: "I would that there were no age between 10 and 3 and 20—or that boys would simply sleep out the rest, for there is nothing in the between but getting wenches with child, wronging the ancestry, stealing and fighting." Kids today are kids nonetheless, and they need caring and connected adults to engage and encourage them—even if we have conveniently forgotten our own youthfulness.

Teaching is a human activity, constrained and made possible by all the limits and potential that characterize any other human activity. Teaching depends on people—people who choose to teach and other people who become students, by choice or not. There are these two sides to teaching, and on each side there are human beings, whole people with their own unique thoughts, hopes, dreams, aspirations, needs, experiences, contexts, agendas, and priorities. Teaching is relational and interactive. It requires dialogue, give and take, back and forth. It is multi-directional. This explains in part why every teaching encounter is particular, each unique in its details.

When Jakob learned to read, for example, he was five years old, a student in my class, and he accomplished this feat without formal instruction. He felt strong and independent and important as a person, and he approached most things with courage and confidence. Reading was no different. He loved hearing stories read, and he had many favorites. He dictated his own stories to accompany pictures he painted. And he could read bits and pieces from his environment: "stop," "pizza," "fruit." One day, he announced he could read. He read a couple of familiar stories, moved on with occasional help, and never looked back. He was reading.

Molly read at six. She watched from a distance when she was in my class as others learned to read, and she looked hard at her own books. She never asked for help, and when help was offered she pushed it away. And then she apparently made a decision that she could do it, that the time had come. She asked me to teach her to read. We sat down and read for two hours. We recognized easy words together and then more difficult ones. We discussed letter sounds and the mystery of phonics. Within a few days she felt like she, too, was a reader.

Shawn learned to read independently at eight, some years after he had been my student. Reading had been a goal for years, but it seemed out of reach to him. He struggled hard to get it, and I struggled to help, both by making him comfortable and by offering a range of reading strategies and opportunities. He found phonics both an incredibly helpful aid and a consistent betrayer. Slowly, painstakingly, he broke the code in the second grade, and read. When he was nine, he was as sophisticated a reader as any of his classmates, and the early frustration was a distant memory.

Each of these learners was different, each had his or her own specific talents, styles, obstacles, and needs. Each demanded a teacher who could invent an appropriate response to a unique encounter.

A powerful, perhaps dominant, view of teaching, holds that teaching is little more than the simple and efficient delivery of curriculum. There is little need for adjustment, no need for dialogue. In this model, teachers are glorified clerks or line employees, functionaries whose job it is to pass along the wisdom and the thinking of some expert, academic, or policy-maker: here is the literary canon; here is the truth of history; here is the skill of reading. The teacher is near the base of the educational hierarchy, just above the student, who is the very bottom of the barrel. Years ago, there was serious talk of making the curriculum "teacher proof," creating packages that even thoughtless, careless people could pass along. The idea behind "new math," for example, was that teachers would transmit something they neither experienced nor understood, and that a generation of brilliant math students would somehow emerge, bypassing teachers altogether. This was, of course, a monumental failure, and that talk has been largely discredited. Today teachers are expected to develop "critical thinking" and "ethical reflection" in youngsters, too often without opportunities to think critically or reflect on values in their own lives. These approaches to reform are folly. The current enthusiasm for some imagined artificial intelligence that will replace the need for thinking, committed teachers in classrooms is only the most recent high-tech version of the old idea of teacher-as-clerk.

I have been a teacher for over thirty years. In that time, I have taught at every level, from preschool to graduate school: I have taught reading, math, and social studies, research methodology and philosophy. I have cared for infants in a day care center and for juvenile "delinquents" in a residential home. In every instance, there has been discovery and surprise, for me as much as for my students. Human relationships are just that way; surprising, idiosyncratic, unique, and marked by variety. Over time, a basic understanding about teaching has emerged and become deeply etched in my own consciousness: Good teaching requires most of all a thoughtful, caring teacher committed to the lives of students. So simple and, in turn, somehow so complicated and so elegant. Like mothering or parenting, good teaching is not a matter of specific techniques or styles, plans or actions. Like friendship, good teaching is not something that can be entirely scripted, preplanned, or prespecified. If a person is thoughtful, caring, and committed, mistakes will be made, but they will not be disastrous; if a person lacks commitment, compassion, or thought, outstanding technique and style will never really compensate. Teaching is primarily a matter of love. The rest is, at best, ornamentation, nice to look at but not of the essence; at worst it is obfuscating—it pulls our attention in the wrong direction and turns us away from the heart of the matter.

Of course, we cannot love what we neither know nor understand. Nor can we teach someone entirely outside our capacity for empathy or comprehension. No one can teach someone they hate, or despise, or find unworthy; someone completely alien or apart from some sense of a shared humanity. On the other hand, sustained interest in and deep knowledge of another person is in itself an act of love, and a good preparation for teaching.

My teacher, Maxine Greene (1973), argues that "the teacher who wishes to be more than a functionary cannot escape the value problem or the difficult matter of moral choice" (p. 181). We recognize, in the first place, how routinely we are made into functionaries. Even as society occasionally posits a romanticized view of the dedicated, caring, inspiring teacher—brilliant, creative, self-sacrificing—we know that the harsh reality in many schools is a structure that disempowers and de-skills, a system that prespecifies each teacher's thoughts and oversees and constrains our activities. In large, impersonal systems, teachers are expected to become obedient, to conform and follow rules—we are expected to deliver the curriculum without much thought, and control the students without much feeling. Students are expected, in turn, to follow the rules and go along with whatever is put before them. The key lessons for everyone in such a school system, top to bottom, are about hierarchy and one's place in it, convention and one's obligation to it, and unquestioning passivity in the face of authority.

We become party to our own depersonalization, then, and to the thoughtlessness of our students; we see ourselves as merely place-holders and low level bureaucrats, filling out forms and completing procedures. Visiting a classroom recently, a teacher welcomed me and added proudly, "We're on page 257 of the math text, exactly where we're supposed to be according to board guidelines." She was, indeed, on page 257, but several students were clearly lost, a few were actually sleeping, and virtually every student in that class was failing math. For this teacher, the received curriculum—certainly not the children and certainly not her own ideas and ideals and worthwhile projects—had become the central thing; powerful, wise, and unchallenged. She was marching through it as instructed, herself a victim of this approach. Everyone was losing—the children through a narrowing of life chances and possibilities; the teacher through a degraded sense of her calling and her work.

Teachers, then, too often implement the initiatives of others; we pass on someone else's ideas of what is valuable to know or experience, and we cultivate a sense of "objectivity" as the greatest good. We become passionless, non-thinking, uninvolved, and we hand over important considerations to "the experts," evading our deepest responsibility and marooning ourselves with the merely technical. As we separate means from ends, we begin to see our students as objects for manipulation. Moral considerations become irrelevant; in the banal language of our time, we are each merely discharging our duties, following orders, simply doing our jobs.

Becoming more than this, resisting this view of teaching is what Greene has in mind when she talks about "the difficult matter of moral choice." She is thinking in part of the ways in which teachers become representatives of adult culture and society to the young, the ways in which we are engaged, sometimes consciously, sometimes unwittingly, in a larger project of inculcating youngsters into a particular social world, a specific set of relationships, "a distinctive way of life." Teachers may have more down-to-earth goals, and the words "socialization" and "acculturation" may seem lofty, alien, or inappropriate to describe classroom reality, but perceived through a larger historical lens, teachers are indeed part of a society's attempt to reproduce itself and stay alive. Teaching is more than transmitting skills; it is a living act, and involves preference and value, obligation and choice, trust and care, commitment and justification.

Hannah Arendt was Maxine Greene's teacher, and she sums it up this way: "Education is the point at which we decide whether we love the world enough to assume responsibility for it and by the same token save it from that ruin which except for renewal, except for the coming of the new and the young, would be inevitable. And education, too, is where we decide whether we love our children enough not to expel them from our world and leave them to their own devices, nor to strike from their hands their chance of undertaking something new, something unforseen by us, but to prepare them in advance for the task of renewing a common world."

Not long ago, for example, a teacher in South Africa would have to consider his or her own classroom experience, the math and science or language arts, her own teaching, but she would also need to be aware of the school system with its strict racial categories and restrictions. The schools, of course, were a part of the system of apartheid, they mirrored it and reproduced it, and so the teacher thought about the larger society outside her school or classroom, and about how it impacted her teaching. If she taught in a school for white children, there was one set of requirements and expectations—a higher set and if she taught in a school for "colored" or African children, different requirements and expectations. The schools passed along the received conventions of the society, and they sorted children according to that particular wisdom. There was in the old South Africa a harsh division in all things, and that division rested on an educational system that offered a small group of white people an education for privilege and power, and the great mass of non-white people an education that would, it was hoped, fit them for lives of exploitation and control. Each South African teacher was expected to pass along the culture's goals and attitudes and aims; each was to play a small part in keeping South African society as it was. Aware of this, each teacher had to wrestle somehow with the problem of values and justifications.

Perhaps this is an extreme example. But if we turn to China or to Poland, Germany, Nicaragua, or Peru, the same problem presents itself. Schools serve societies in all kinds of direct and indirect ways. Societies set up schools as institutional forms for the re-creation of specific values and norms, dispositions and assumptions. Teachers must somehow warrant these larger social goals and values in order to teach easily and comfortably; if they cannot, then they must find ways to teach in an alternative way, perhaps as an act of resistance. This is one reason why the schools in South Africa, and elsewhere, are such pivotal points of struggle; why students and teachers have been so active and public in their opposition to government policies; and why school reform is such a regular part of our own landscape. Schools are one important place where we fight out notions of the good and the right.

There is no American exception, and the problem is as real in the United States as it is anywhere. Of course, this is a time of intense doubt and confusion in our own society, of fundamental questioning and serious reconsideration. It is a time of changing roles and expectations and a time of conflicting demands on schools and teachers. While uncertainty and upheaval may encourage a tendency to seek solace in easy answers, those answers—those references to convention or precedent or higher authority—in many instances simply will not hold. The teacher must find ways to choose and to act in a shifting, uncertain world. She must find ways to take responsibility for her teaching without guarantees. This, as we shall see, requires a teacher to be wide-awake and fully present in her teaching; it requires a kind of heroism in the classroom.

The teacher who embraces the "difficult matter of moral choice" is thrust face to face with students in a classroom. At some level she has already addressed a fundamental ethical question, for she has chosen the task of encouraging and empowering others. This is so because whatever subject or discipline or approach she follows, she is engaged in an activity designed (by someone's definition) to improve or enable or endow others. All teaching, consciously or unconsciously, explicitly or implicitly, deals, therefore, with two questions: What knowledge and experiences are most worthwhile? And, what are the means to strengthen, invigorate, and enable each person to take full advantage of those worthwhile experiences and that valuable knowledge?

Of course, neither question has an easy, straightforward or universal answer for every individual in every situation. The dizzying diversity of human experience and capacity alone demands that teachers look deeply at our students, that we see them as creatures like ourselves, and yet unique in important ways. This is a central challenge of teaching, and it is essentially a moral challenge; it cannot be resolved by referring to fact or to empirical data alone. There is no single, provable answer. There are several possible answers, and infinite possible courses of action to follow. We are left to think about what ought to be and what ought not to be; we are left to investigate and inquire into and with our students, and to interrogate the larger contexts of our teaching; we are left to choose among conflicting claims, and this requires thinking critically and intensely about possible courses and outcomes. If we teachers want our students to acquire the knowledge, skills, and dispositions of mind that will allow them to live fully and well, to be strong and capable and competent, and to have the capacity to shape their individual and collective destinies, then we must struggle to figure out how to realize these lofty goals in specific situations with particular students. When do we focus our efforts on teaching what we consider necessary skills, and when do we allow students to act and to initiate? When do we nurture and hold close, and when do we let go? How do we know when we are doing the right thing?

For Greene, the answer lies in teachers learning how to "do philosophy." She means that teachers can approach teaching and learning critically and deliberately. They can struggle to stay conscious and alive, resisting the merely routine. They can use the findings of social scientists, for example, not as universal truths, but as something to be examined, considered, contemplated. It means they can hold even their own experiences as tentative, contingent, and open to question. "Doing philosophy" means being self-aware and highly conscious of the world around us. And it means attending again and again to a fundamental teaching question: "Given what I now know (about the world, about this class, about this student before me), what should I do?" As Greene (1973) says:

> Involved individuals have to make the moral choices which are ordinarily specific. The more sensitive teachers are to the demands of the process of justification, the more explicit they are about the norms that govern their actions, the more personally engaged they are in assessing surrounding circumstances and potential consequences, the more "ethical" they will be; and we cannot ask much more. (p. 221)

Nel Noddings (1986) helps, too, by arguing that teachers can be aided in the "difficult matter of moral choice" if they can adopt an "ethic of caring." For Noddings, the central issue is not following a specific duty or principle, but rather being true in a direct, immediate sense to people with whom one has a relationship:

> Natural caring—the sort of response made when we want to care for another [a loved one, a baby, a sick friend] establishes the ideal for ethical caring, and ethical caring imitates the ideal in its efforts to institute, maintain or reestablish natural caring. . . . Persons guided by an ethic of caring do not ask whether it is their duty to be faithful . . . rather, for them fidelity to persons is fidelity; indeed, fidelity is a quality of the relation and not merely an attribute of an individual moral agent's behavior or character. (p. 385)

This points us in the direction of the whole person. From the perspective of an ethic of caring it is the person before us who becomes our central concern. This in no way implies a lack of concern for academic rigor or excellence, or for teaching basic skills, but it does mean that skills are taught, for example, as a result of concern for the person, that is, that the "one is undertaken in light of the other" (p. 387). I insist that my students learn algebra because of my love of them, not of it.

The challenge of teaching is to decide who you want to be as a teacher, what you care about and what you value, and how you will conduct yourself in classrooms with students. It is to name yourself as a teacher, knowing that institutional realities will only enable that goal in part (if at all) and that the rest is up to you. It is to choose the rocky road of change. It is to move beyond the world as we find it with its conventional patterns and its received wisdom in pursuit of a world and a reality that could be, but is not yet.

It is, furthermore, to choose to do something that enables the choices of others, that supports the human impulse to grow. In this sense it is to choose teaching not as a job only, and not even as a career or a profession. It is to choose teaching as a project or a vocation, something one is called to do. In a vocation like teaching there is a vital link between private and public worlds, between personal fulfillment and social responsibility. There is also a sense of commitment and purpose that rejects the measured calculation that pervades so much of work today. Teaching is the vocation of vocations, because to choose teaching is to choose to enable the choices of others. It is to be about the business of empowerment, the business of enabling others to choose well. There are all kinds of skills, tools, dispositions, and opportunities required for these broad choices to be made, and teachers must somehow become responsible for all of it.

Because society is indifferent and because we as members of society are floating in a kind of purposelessness, it is easy to dismiss talk of ethical action as romantic, foolish, or even quaint. This image of quaintness is intensified in schools increasingly bent toward a narrow agenda of efficiency and control. But we need to talk of values—of what ought to be—if we are ever to really understand ourselves, our situations, and our options, and if we are ever to undertake meaningful action toward improvement in schools or in society. The problems we face today are not essentially technical or material problems; they are, at their heart, moral problems.

Teaching is an act of hope for a better future. The rewards of teaching are neither ostentatious nor obvious—they are often internal, invisible, and of the moment. But paradoxically, they can be deeper, more lasting, and less illusory than the cut of your clothes or the size of your home. The rewards of teaching might include watching a youngster make a connection and come alive to a particular literacy, discipline, or way of thinking, or seeing another child begin to care about something or someone in a way that he never cared before, or observing a kid become a person of values because you treated her as a valuable person. There is a particularly powerful satisfaction in caring in a time of carelessness, and of thinking for yourself in a time of thoughtlessness. The reward of teaching is knowing that your life makes a difference.

2

SEEING THE STUDENT

Teaching is an interactive practice that begins and ends with seeing the student. This is more complicated than it seems, for it is something that is ongoing and never completely finished. The student grows and changes, the teacher learns, the situation shifts, and seeing becomes an evolving challenge. As layers of mystification and obfuscation are peeled away, as the student becomes more fully present to the teacher, experiences and ways of thinking and knowing that were initially obscure become the ground on which an authentic and vital teaching practice can be constructed.

Our youngest child came into our family when he was fourteen months old—unexpected, unannounced. Chesa was set adrift when his biological parents—close, long-time friends of ours—could no longer care for him. His grandparents kept him for a short time, and then he came to us.

For a long time, he was an easy child—agreeable, eager to please, perhaps a bit compliant. He was never fussy, never demanding. On the other side, he never displayed much enthusiasm: His play lacked commitment and his explorations of the world were tentative. He watched his new brothers at play, one of them almost four years older, and the other just half a year older, but he joined in rather reluctantly. He was subject to every sore throat and ear infection that came near him, and both his physical strength and his affect seemed always at low ebb. He was downcast, depressed. Later his depression gave way to an explosive anger, often self-directed. He was clumsy, both physically and socially, and he would frequently crash into people and things—often hurting himself or angering others—and afterwards genuinely wonder what had happened.

Chesa also had qualities that could help him negotiate and take control of his life. One was a dogged determination—a willingness to work and work and work at a task or a challenge until he succeeded. During a fund-raiser for his swim team, he swam lap after graceless lap, the slowest on the team but also the last to emerge from the water. When his mind was set, he never gave up and he never gave in, no matter what. Another quality was his keen intelligence and his steel-trap memory. His report of events or conversations was filled with color, nuance, and detail. Finally, he could be incredibly compassionate and unexpectedly generous. Each of these qualities, of course, could be experienced in two ways: his iron will could be seen as stubbornness or resoluteness; his memory as acute or obsessive; his sweetness as strong or weak.

As he set off for first grade we were painfully aware of the many ways Chesa might be experienced, of the many ways he could be seen as a student. There was his obstinacy, for example. There was the matter of anger and temper and the highly visible issue of plowing into people. Who would his teacher see coming through the door? How would she know our wonderful child?

We were lucky. Chesa's teacher was a young man named Kevin Sweeney who admired his strengths and quickly figured out interesting and clever ways to leverage these against his weaknesses. For example, he gave Chesa cleaning tasks almost every day—not the routine stuff, but tasks that tapped into his work-horse nature. "Chesa, could you wash these shelves this afternoon? Just move the paper over here and then use a bucket of soapy water and a sponge." This not only focused Chesa on a goal, but it made a worthwhile quality more visible to the other children and to himself, and this, in turn, made him a stronger, more accepted group member. Furthermore, it provided the teacher with a steady reminder of something to value in Chesa, a challenging child for much of the day.

All of this came back to me when I was working with a group of ten-year-old boys in an inner city public school. I showed them a simple structure for writing a brief, autobiographical sketch or poem. The first line is your first name, followed by a line of three words that describe you to yourself. The next line is something you love, then something you hate, something you fear, and something you wish for. The last line is your last name. I gave the kids an example:

I am Martin
   courageous non-violent warrior
   I love all people
   I hate oppression
   I am afraid of ignorance
   I wish for freedom
King.

Hannibal pointed out that I had left out "Luther," which was right, so we made the last line, "Luther King." Now they made poems for themselves:

> I am Hannibal
>   fluky but funny
>   I love the Bulls
>   I hate being whipped
>   I am afraid of Freddy
>   I wish for Michael Jordan to come over
> Johnson.

> I am Aaron
>   small, black, frightened
>   I love my mom
>   I hate being picked on
>   I am afraid of the raper man and the police
>   I wish for happiness
> Blackwell.

When I had asked his teacher if Aaron could join me for an hour on this morning, as he had on other occasions, she had practically pushed him out the door. "He's no good today," she had said. "His mind is wandering and he doesn't want to work." Now I looked at Aaron again. He was small, frail really, and he did look frightened. He smiled a lot, but always apologetically, looking down, unsure. He was quiet, never initiating talk or play, always reacting. His face was streaked, his hair uncombed, and his eyes were puffy and resting on large dark circles. I wondered: Why is Aaron frightened? Who are the police in his life? What is the happiness he wishes for?

As we talked about his poem and about some of my questions, I learned that the raper man was a large character in his life, someone Aaron could describe physically, even though he had never seen him. The raper man had huge hands and was ugly, with big, red bumps on his face. He drove an old, wrecked car, and he was often sighted by other children on the walk from school to home, so Aaron and his little sister mainly ran home each day. The police loomed large: While he didn't know any of them himself, two of his brothers had had frequent encounters with the law. Aaron told me a long story about one brother, James, who had been falsely accused of gang membership and arrested in a playground for "just being there." Aaron had visited James yesterday in Cook County Jail, he told me, and today

James would go on trial for first-degree murder. "My mom says maybe he'll come home this week if the judge sees he didn't do it."

No wonder his teacher said: "He's no good today. His mind is wandering and he doesn't want to work." I ask myself if I'd be any good with my own brother on trial for murder, or if I could concentrate on work sheets with all this going on. And then I think of his mother, and I wonder what her hopes are for Aaron in school. I think of her in light of our hopes for Chesa, and of our good fortune in having him known and understood by Kevin Sweeney. What could this mother tell any teacher about Aaron that would be of use? Would the teacher or anyone else in the school care? Would they find a way to teach him?

———————————

When we teachers look out over our classrooms, what do we see? Half-civilized barbarians? Savages? A collection of deficits, or IQs, or averages? Do we see fellow creatures? We see students in our classrooms, of course, but who are they? What hopes do they bring? What is the language of their dreams? What experiences have they had, and where do they want to go? What interests or concerns them, how have they been hurt, what are they frightened of, what will they fight for, and what and whom do they care about? What is their bliss? Their pain?

When I began teaching, we were told that many of our students were "culturally deprived." This became a strong, germinal idea for some teachers, and cultural deprivation was being unearthed and remediated all over the place. We assumed it was an actual condition, like freckles, that was a piece of some kids. It didn't take long, however, for cultural deprivation as a concept to come in for some serious and sustained questioning: Is calling someone "culturally deprived" the same as calling them not white, not middle class? Is Spanish a "lower" language than English? Is the implication, then, that some cultures are superior and others inferior? Or that some children have a culture and others do not? What is culture anyway? In time, the concept of cultural deprivation was discredited as patronizing and untrue, and it fell into disuse.

Unhappily, labeling students has become even more widespread in the intervening years—it is an epidemic in our schools, a toxic habit with no known limits. It's as if supervisors, coordinators, and administrators have nothing better to do than to mumble knowingly about "soft signs," "attention deficit disorder," or "low impulse control," and all the rest of us stand around smiling, pretending to know what they're talking about. The categories keep splintering and proliferating, getting nuttier as they go: L.D., B.D., E.H., T.A.G., E.M.H. It's almost impossible for teachers today not to see before them "gifted and talented" students, "learning disabled" youngsters, and children "at risk." I recently asked a scholar who had just presented a major research paper at a professional conference on "at-risk" students to give me a brief definition of "at-risk," using, I insisted, only "Peter Rabbit English." He said flatly, "Black or Hispanic, poor, and from a single-parent household." "At risk" is simply "cultural deprivation" recycled for today. And, most important, "at risk" is no one's self-definer—I've worked in tough situations forever, and never met a kid who said, "Hi, I'm Maria, and I'm at risk."

The problem is this: in the human-centered act of teaching, all attempts to create definitive categories lower our sights, misdirect our vision, and mislead our intentions. Labels are limiting. They offer a single lens concentrated on a specific deficit when what we need are multiple ways of seeing a child's ever-changing strengths. All the categories are upside down—they conceal more than they reveal. They are abstract, when what we need is immediate and concrete. The focusing questions for effective teachers must be these: Who is this person before me? What are his interests and areas of wonder? How does she express herself and what is her awareness of herself as a learner? What effort and potential does she bring? These are the kinds of questions we need to attend to.

If I were to brainstorm a list of things I can't do or can't do well, things I don't understand or care about, activities that make me seem incompetent or feel ridiculous, I could fill a chalkboard in just a few seconds. Let's see: I can't type or use the computer, I can't speak French, I don't fish, I can't fix the car, I can't play tennis, I don't understand golf, I don't know how a television works, I can't read music, I'm lousy at chess, I can't play the trumpet, I can't repair the refrigerator, and on and on. Most of these would be useful things to know; each could, in fact, be interesting and worthwhile.

Now imagine some school administrator or teacher constructing a curriculum to correct these deficiencies in me. I might attend remedial auto shop three mornings a week, resource room refrigerator maintenance and TV repair on alternate days, take the slow French class every afternoon, and so on. The goal may well be to make me a

more skilled and a better person, but the result would likely be alien-
ation, disinterest, and failure. You see, I have no interest in learning
to fix cars. I simply don't care about it. I don't own a TV and have
no burning desire to know how they work. I have no particular skill
in refrigeration, no particular aptitude in foreign language or music.
Most of this curriculum would be distant from me, and some of it
would even frighten me—the tennis lessons, for example, would make
me look like a fool in front of my classmates. All in all this attempt to
fix me would likely make me feel bad, and could well drive me completely away from school.

The list of my deficiencies (dramatically shortened here to preserve some shred of self-respect) is, of course, true but inadequate.
There is no distinction, for example, between items that might intimidate but also attract and fascinate me, like using the computer, and
items that hold absolutely no allure, like golf or fishing. Furthermore,
this list tells you very little of importance about me. You don't know,
for example, that I ride my bicycle to work every day and that I know
a lot about bikes. You don't know that I love movies and jazz and
baseball. You don't know that I am a good baker and an excellent,
inventive cook, nor that I cook like I teach, with some broad framework of planning but without strict recipes. You don't know that I
found some nice baby eggplants at the market yesterday, and that I
let them lead me into dinner—and that only afterwards could I construct a recipe for interested guests, explaining how the eggplant made
me think of ginger, and how I then found some garlic and an onion,
a bottle of old wine, and so on.

Not only does the list of incompetencies fail to tell you anything
of what I know or care about, it also doesn't tell you anything about
my temperament or disposition of mind—that I tend to be supportive
and nurturing, for example, and that I am an intrepid (sometimes
meddling) interpersonal problem solver. It doesn't tell you anything
about how I learn—that I read slowly, for example, and retain only
what I have told someone else. As I look at it, the deficiencies list tells
you almost nothing about me—about my experiences, needs, dreams,
fears, skills, or know-how—and as a teacher it provides you with information of only distant, peripheral value. It doesn't offer you any insight or clues into how you might engage me in a journey of learning,
or how you might invite me into your classroom as a student. In
short, the list fails to answer the key question: Given what I know
now, how shall I teach this person?

Finally, the list makes me feel rotten as a learner. I want to feel
strong and healthy, secure, independent, connected as a worthwhile

member of the group. When these qualities are nurtured and supplied with opportunity, I can act with surprising courage—I can take criticism, be a good ally to others, face up to my shortcomings and failures, keep going against all odds, experiment in new realms. In other words, my ability to exercise my mind with hope and sureness is linked to my emotional state, my feelings, my affect. When they are disregarded, I—like most people—hold back, cringe a bit, and the possibility of a productive formal education narrows.

In the odd, often upside-down world of schools, we typically start in the wrong place. We start with what kids can't do and don't know. It's as if we brainstormed a list for each of them as I did for myself, that we figured out what they don't understand or value, what they feel incompetent or insecure about, and we then developed a curriculum to remediate each deficiency. The curriculum is built on a deficit-model; it is built on repairing weakness. And it simply doesn't work.

It isn't that educators don't mean well. Youngsters do indeed need access to certain literacies and skills if they are to function fully and well in our society. And it isn't as if there are no students who learn: Children are learning all the time, and not just what we think we are teaching them. The irony is that the students who tend to succeed in school learn in spite of—not because of—our treatments. And those who fail in school are subject to the most relentless and concentrated attack on their weaknesses—seemingly to no avail.

The framework for the almighty lesson plan—that daily, classroom-level reminder of this whole approach—neatly embodies the deficit approach: It is linear, one-directional, incremental, and entirely outside the student. Lesson plans typically begin with behavioral objectives, as in, "Students will understand vowel blends," or "Students will multiply double-digit numbers." They then describe the materials needed, the activities that will occur, and how it all fits together within some larger plan. It is all very neat, all seemingly objective. The problem is that this has nothing to do with how people learn, it never captures the complexity of classroom life nor the idiosyncratic, tumultuous individual pathways to knowledge. Students will understand vowel blends? How about Eric, in the back of the class? He's thinking about what he's going to do later when he sees Brian. How about James, ambling aimlessly to the pencil sharpener again? He never does well in reading or on these work sheets anyway. The teacher experiences the problems but feels somewhat trapped: "I've got thirty other children, and I have to think of everyone, not just those not doing well. I try to work with them individually when I can, of course, but they have to make some effort. In any case their grades will reflect both their efforts and what they have learned." Exactly. Eric and James already know they are bad students, they are already drifting, and all of this is simply confirmation. Operating, as it does, without reference to the students themselves, this deficiency-driven approach is self-justifying and closed: Some will learn and some will not, some will work hard and others won't, some will make it and some will fall away. It's all quite predictable.

If this conclusion is objectionable—and I believe it is entirely unacceptable to those of us engaged in teaching as a moral act, or teaching as an intellectual challenge—there must be another approach. We must find ways to break with the deficit-driven model, and we must move away from teaching as a way of attacking incompetencies, teaching as uncovering perceived deficiencies and constructing micro-units for repair. We must find a better way, a way that builds on strengths, experiences, skills, and abilities; a way that engages the whole person and guides that person to greater fulfillment and power. I am reminded of the plea of a Native American parent whose five-year-old son had been labeled a "slow learner": "Wind-Wolf knows the names and migration patterns of more than forty birds. He knows there are thirteen tail feathers on a perfectly balanced eagle. What he needs is a teacher who knows his full measure" (Lake, 1990, p. 48).

―――――――

Most teachers want to know the full measure of their students. We want to understand what motivates them and makes them tick, what engages and interests them, and we want to know why they act as they do. We want to be more effective—to maximize those satisfying moments when we reach children, and minimize the frustrations of seeing everything we try fall flat. And while we have become accustomed to scores and grades, we often want to know more than we can possibly learn by relying on an objective, impersonal standard, whether it be a grade-level average, a test result, or a letter or number assigned to potential or achievement.

Teachers need to be one part detective: We sift the clues children leave, follow the leads, and diligently uncover the facts in order to fill out and make credible the story of their growth and development. We need to be one part researcher: collecting data, analyzing information, testing hypotheses. Teachers need to be one part world-class puzzle master, painstakingly fitting together the tiny pieces of some mammoth, intricate jigsaw of childhood. And we need to be all of this with a significant difference: Our story never ends with a neat conclusion, our data is mostly unruly and insufficient, and our jigsaw puzzle is always incomplete because it is always fluid, always changing. Whatever truths we discover are contingent; our facts are tentative. This is because we are interested in children—living, breathing, squirming, growing, moving, messy, idiosyncratic children. Just when we have gained some worthwhile insight, just when we have captured some interesting essence, the children change, the kaleidoscope turns, and we must look again, even more deeply.

We must find a way, too, to ground our observations in many dimensions at once: intellectual, cultural, physical, spiritual, emotional. In looking more deeply, we must try to see beyond our own stereotypes and prejudices, beyond some notion of how children ought to behave filtered through smoky, uncritical childhood memory. We must see beyond the unstated assumption driving most schools, the wacky idea that children are puny, inadequate adults and that the job of education is to transport them as quickly as possible from that sorry state. We must look unblinkingly at the way children really are, and struggle to make sense of everything that we see in order to teach them.

Theories of child development, including developmental psychology, can help by reminding us that childhood is a unique, distinct time and place in the growth of a person. Jean Piaget, for example, can alert us to the ways in which young children's thinking is concrete and immediate compared with the thinking of older children; Erik Erikson can underline the importance of identity and broadening group affiliation for adolescents. We can notice the ways that human meanings shift qualitatively as we grow. We need to remember, certainly, that childhood has its own validity, that it is not simply a functional stage or a preparation for life; that a child's life is a full life nonetheless. Perhaps most important, theorists like Piaget—if we take his method seriously—can demonstrate the power of intense observation, careful questioning, respectful listening and detailed record keeping in our quest to understand the child. Too often we accept theory as doctrine—we speak a half-language of slogans and formulas. We become immunized against complexity, or worse, we use developmental theory to build a curriculum designed to hurry children through the "stages of development," thereby abandoning, for example, Piaget's fascination with how the child knows. In this way, child development, too, becomes dogma, another obstacle in our attempt to accurately see the student.

Observing children purposefully and carefully is a way to get to know them, a way to look more deeply. We need as full and realistic a picture as possible of the child in motion—interacting, choosing, constructing, learning, responding, functioning. That picture will be an action shot, probably a little blurry around the edges but a picture that can strengthen the teacher's ability to teach. While groups certainly have their own rhythms, patterns, and demands, observations of individual children are essential. Observing individual children helps us to keep in mind that each child is different, and each is his or her own universe.

Here, for example, are classroom notes I made about a student over several months:

Ashley is a delightful child, rewarding to work with, an enthusiastic, energetic three-year-old. She has an expressive face and body, big dark eyes, round cheeks, malleable features. When she laughs, her whole body releases and roars. When she cries she is convulsed with sobs from head to foot. When she clowns, she's a cartoon.

Ashley is small-boned, a well-coordinated runner and climber, strong, agile, and healthy. She meets the world with all her senses—tasting the sand, painting her face, smelling the clay and then squeezing it between her fingers, scooping the fish out of the tank—operating out of a strong bodily base.

Ashley spends a large part of the day in dramatic play—sometimes with the blocks, sometimes in the dress-up area, and often just spontaneously while reading or painting. At lunch one day recently, Ashley sat with Kate. Each child had brought a doll to the table. Ashley turned to Kate and said, "Here, baby, eat your cereal." She held out a spoonful of apple sauce, which Kate took into her mouth. Ashley smiled and started to feed Kate, stroking her hair lightly and watching her intently, face tipped downward, eyebrows raised, speaking in an exaggerated, patronizing voice: "Good baby. Eat your cereal." Kate was willing, and after lunch Ashley took her hand and led her off to brush her teeth.

At the sand table another morning she played with four or five kids for twenty minutes. Her body was relaxed and loose as she leaned forward over the edge, balancing on one foot, her mouth relaxed, lips slightly parted. "This is tea," she said scooping sand into a large cup and then pouring it out. "Now here's an egg," not speaking to anyone in particular. Later: "Now I made rice and beans." Finally she drifted away and went to the record player. She put on the record "Annie" and sang "Tomorrow" by herself, swaying in front of the record player, acting, spreading her arms wide and affecting a performing style.

Ashley is often the first to arrive. One day she dashed easily into the room, smiling and shouting my name: "Bill." She wheeled around beaming to her mother and patted Kathy's pregnant belly, repeating "Bill! Bill!"

"What do you have there?"

"My baby!" she shouted and exploded in laughter.

"You can hold it, Bill."

This was new, because for weeks she had said that no one could hold the new baby when it arrived.

She slithered out of her coat and skipped once around the room, looking at the bagels and butter on the table, touching the turtle, tapping an easel. She returned and sat on a chair near where Kathy was unpacking her things.

"Put my shoes on, mama," she said matter-of-factly.

"I'm busy," said Kathy, "but I'll be with you in a minute. Why don't you loosen the laces to your boots?"

Ashley did this agreeably, concentrating hard. After her mother helped her on with her soft shoes she hopped to the table and took a hearty bite of a bagel. "Mmm, butter," she crooned.

Kathy said goodbye and left. "Bye, bye," Ashley called after her. Arrivals haven't always been easy. Sometimes Ashley cries and wants to be held, but Kathy is always direct and easy with her, following a consistent pattern every day.

Soon two others arrived and joined her at the table. She said hello to each, then nodding she said: "You can hold my baby, José. And especially Asha can hold it." The other two seem oblivious to the treasure that they have been offered.

When the bagels were done, she cried out: "Let's go up here." She flew to the ladder and gracefully pulled herself up to the loft. She quickly assembled a square of blocks with a window. She concentrated hard and didn't seem to notice two more arrivals, even though one parent was insistent on praising her work. After ten minutes she called out, "Hey, Asha. The spaceship is ready." Three kids joined her and she gave them each some colored cubes and said, "Here are the batteries," and demonstrated how she wanted them put into the windows.

One day several kids were tracing their hands on white paper and coloring them in. Ashley carefully colored her hand brown, intent on filling in all the spaces. When she was done she flipped the paper over and drew two large hand-like shapes, leaving one white and coloring the other black. "This is Jim," she said pointing to the white hand, "and this is Kathy."

Ashley is intently interested in color and race. Her mother is Jamaican and black, her father is Jewish and white. For a long time, her favorite book was Black is Brown is Tan, a children's book about an interracial family, and she called it, "My book."

She recently asked one of the teachers what color he was. The teacher replied: "What do you think?"

"No, No, I asked you first."

"OK, I'm white," he said. She then asked about several kids, black and white, and he answered each time. At the end she said contentedly, "Yep, you got them all right."

Ashley often ties a piece of yarn into her hair and calls it her ponytail, "Just like Sarah's." Last week she said Kathy wasn't her mother because Kathy looks just like her friend Abdul.
"Mommy found me in a store and liked me so she bought me." She was serious and intent, trying it out.

Later she asked me: "Do you know what color my new baby will be?"

"I think so."

"Brown, just like me."

Attending to the details of one child at a time can develop a richer understanding of that person, of course, and it can simultaneously strengthen a deeper and more powerful understanding of all children, for it sensitizes teachers to detail, to their own ability to observe and understand, and to similarities and differences between children. Child observation is especially important in situations where structures obscure our vision and depersonalize students, where classes are large, for example, paper work, forms, and standardized ways of looking at kids entrenched, and where teachers have no regular, formal way of discussing children together.

The goal of observation is understanding, not some imagined objectivity. If a teacher is invested in and fascinated by a child—if the child is a "favorite"—this is not a problem. The teacher will always be working to understand and teach that child. The problem is when the child is unseen, invisible, or not cared for—and this is not a problem of objectivity but of commitment. Pushing oneself to see and observe and understand this child—and every child—is an act of compassion and an important part of teaching.

Interpretation has as big a place in observing children as description does: One tells more about the speaker, the other more about the child, but both are necessary. Self-awareness and knowing students are both part of the intellectual challenge of teaching. Here are classroom notes I made, around the same time, on two other students:

José and Abdul are the roughhousers, disrupters, firecrackers. It is common to see them roaring from the loft to the book area, through the art area, around the room and back to the loft, knocking things over, yelling and chasing.

Between them, José is the leader, often the aggressor and the energizer. He is not the least activity-oriented, but seems mainly to be involved, even in his calmer moments, in exploring the space, touching, discarding, moving on, touching something else. José is a gate-keeper, constantly protecting his and Abdul's relationship by hitting, pushing, telling kids, "you aren't our friend," fighting to sit next to Abdul at lunch. Often, if Abdul initiates a block-building project, José will stand at the head of the stairs, his legs and arms spread to keep everyone out, literally guarding the gate.

Abdul loves José, waits for him quietly each day and lights up when he comes bursting in. When José doesn't come, Abdul is quiet, gentle and cooperative. He seems innocent enough, very sweet and wide-eyed. He'll play with several kids until José comes; then it is only José and him, which is the way José wants it.

José and Abdul are not a popular leadership group, except at times like rest time when they tap a group nerve and can lead a general uprising. I remember kids like José from my childhood; I had boundless admiration for someone who could be so uninhibited and so irreverent. They're both adorable.

For all children, it is better to have a caring, self-aware teacher who is haphazard when it comes to record-keeping than a detailed and particular record-keeper who is careless about kids. Nevertheless, beyond a lot of informal "taking in" of the child, more formal observations and record-keeping can be of enormous value. This takes time, but it is not impossible, even in large groups. And it is not necessarily time away from teaching; it can be built centrally into the structure of the day. Some teachers keep a pad and pencil handy so that they can jot notes during the day to be filled in outside of school; others have a tape recorder available for quick observations. Vivian Gussin Paley, a teacher who has documented her classroom experiences through an impressive series of books over several years, uses and reuses a single cassette, which she calls her "disciplinarian," a technique that pushes her to transcribe and make sense of material soon after it is recorded. Taking a moment to step back from the group and focus on one student, keeping a running record of everything that that student does while solving a problem, working with some material, or interacting with others can yield a rich harvest of information about learning style, preference and approach, maturity, and disposition of mind.

Much of the time of record-keeping is time outside of school, it is time in the evenings or on the weekends. It is useful for some teachers to keep a journal or diary, to have a daily record of memorable events and reflections. Again there is no pretense of constructing an objective record; the goal, instead, is to create an instrument for thinking about teaching and children in a critical, sustained way. Not only is the journal an instrument for thinking and planning and harvesting ideas, but, over time, a journal will contain many little pieces about this or that child, bits that can be brought together when seeking a deeper understanding of growth and development, or when preparing to discuss this child with parents or colleagues. It is useful, as well, to write anecdotal records every week concerning ten or fifteen students. Again, over several weeks a teacher can gather a lot of information—including, for example, which students are not noticed; who might be falling through the cracks.

It is useful, if understanding students is a central goal, to afford children multiple opportunities to choose, to initiate, to create during some part of classroom life. This might take the form of "choice time" in a primary classroom, a time when children can decide which activity to pursue and the teacher can observe the various choices and make a few brief notes on the work of particular kids as they pursue their interests. In a classroom of older students, this might take the form of a project time, an independent research time, a free-reading time, or simply a break time, when youngsters can talk among themselves. Again, the teacher can note choices made and approaches to work, play, and relationship.

———————

Parents are a powerful, usually underutilized source of knowledge about youngsters. Parents are too often made to feel unwelcome in schools, and we too often dismiss their insights as subjective and overly involved. In fact, the insights of parents—urgent, invested, passionate, immediate—are exactly what we need. Here, for example, is a letter to a teacher from a Native American mother whose son is about to start school (this has been copied and passed widely among educators, but has not, to my knowledge, been published, and the author is unknown):

> Before you take charge of the classroom that contains my child, please ask yourself why you are going to teach Indian children. What are your expectations? What rewards do you anticipate? . . .
>
> Write down and examine all the information and opinions you possess about Indians. What are the stereotypes and untested assumptions that you bring with you into the classroom? How many negative attitudes towards Indians will you put before my child? . . .
>
> Too many teachers, unfortunately, seem to see their role as rescuer. My child does not need to be rescued; he does not consider being Indian a misfortune. He has a culture, probably older than yours; he has meaningful values and a rich and varied experiential background. However strange or incomprehensible it may seem to you, you have no right to do or say anything that implies to him that it is less than satisfactory . . .
>
> Like most Indian children his age, he is competent. He can dress himself, prepare a meal for himself, clean up afterwards, care for a younger child. He knows his Reserve, all of which is his home, like the back of his hand.
>
> He is not accustomed to having to ask permission to do the ordinary things that are part of normal living. He is seldom forbidden to do anything; more usually the consequences of an action are explained to him, and he is allowed to decide for himself whether or not to act. His entire existence since he has been old enough to see and hear has been an experiential learning situation, arranged to provide him with the opportunity to develop his skills and confidence in his own capacities. Didactic teaching will be an alien experience for him . . .
>
> He has been taught, by precept, that courtesy is an essential part of human conduct and rudeness is any action that makes another person feel stupid or foolish. Do not mistake his patient courtesy for indifference or passivity.
>
> He doesn't speak standard English, but he is in no way "linguistically handicapped." If you will take the time and courtesy to listen and observe carefully, you will see that he and the other Indian children communicate very well, both among themselves

and with other Indians. They speak "functional" English, very effectively augmented by their fluency in the silent language, the subtle, unspoken communication of facial expressions, gestures, body movement, and the use of personal space.

You will be well advised to remember that our children are skillful interpreters of the silent language. They will know your feelings and attitudes with unerring precision, no matter how carefully you arrange your smile or modulate your voice. They will learn in your classroom, because children learn involuntarily. What they learn will depend on you.

Will you help my child to learn to read, or will you teach him that he has a reading problem? Will you help him develop problem solving skills, or will you teach him that school is where you try to guess what answer the teacher wants?

Will he learn that his sense of his own value and dignity is valid, or will he learn that he must forever be apologetic and "trying harder" because he isn't white? Can you help him acquire the intellectual skills he needs without at the same time imposing your values on top of those he already has?

Respect my child. He is a person. He has a right to be himself.

Inviting letters from parents is one way to learn from them. Another is to structure opportunities for them to be powerful in their access to school, the classroom, and the teacher. For example, I have always given parents of my students my phone number and address, something that colleagues sometimes considered unwise in big city schools where parents are often seen as the enemy. I found ways to socialize with parents outside of school and to bring them into class as tutors, aids, and experts. Everyone, after all, is an expert on his or her own life; many are also experts at something interesting but not available in the conventional curriculum—carving, sewing, playing mah jong. Bringing parents into focus can be useful to youngsters and also to teachers—after all, we cannot really be child-centered if we are not also family-centered. Perhaps most important, I discovered early on that I had to structure parent-teacher conferences in a way that challenged the sense of cringing anticipation that usually pervades those encounters. I did this by beginning the first conference with a simple opening: "You know more about your child than I can ever hope to know; what advice can you give me to make me a better teacher for her?" Turning the power relationship upside down, inviting information and emotion, becoming student to their aspirations, fears, and experiences, I would usually become a more qualified teacher for their child as well.

———————————

The strongest source of knowledge about the student remains the student herself, and tapping into that knowledge is not so difficult. Kids love to tell us about themselves, and we can structure multiple opportunities for them to do so. I have always asked children to draw their families, for example. Young children tend to draw little tadpole creatures, while older youngsters work hard to represent with greater accuracy. But in either case, they reveal a lot: this family includes a dog, a grandmother, and Aunt Helen; this family has grown up children and in-laws, nieces, and nephews; this family has a large figure who is "mom" and a little tiny "dad" in the corner of the page; this family visits their father in prison.

We might do autobiographical sketches like the "I am Aaron" poem described earlier. The children might draw or write about the worst thing they ever ate, or the scariest moment of their lives, or the sweetest person they ever knew, or their best friends. If we're reading a story and a character does something courageous or cowardly, generous or small, we will almost certainly take the time to describe when some of us saw someone be generous or cowardly, or when we ourselves were. We might move toward deeper autobiographical writing, family trees, or keeping journals or diaries.

One useful homework assignment I have regularly given to preschoolers and college students alike is to have them research their first names: How did you come to have your name? What was the thought behind it? Who gave it to you? Every name has a story, even if only that it sounded nice with the last name. I have pursued names to the Bible and to the Koran, to Russia, China, Brazil, and Puerto Rico, to grandma, great-uncle, and a dead cousin, to Eugene Debs, Malcolm X, and Abraham Lincoln. In one kindergarten class we had a Marcus (from Marcus Garvey), a Solomon (from the Old Testament), and a Lolita (from Lolita Lebron). We also had a Veronica, "because my dad loves Archie comics and always said if he had a girl he'd name her Veronica." She brought in some comics so we could understand her name better. Names are powerful for individuals, and they sometimes have powerful stories worked up in them as well.

When we discuss culture in class, I have asked students to bring in a "cultural artifact" from home. Again a world of importance opens up: religious symbols, a book, military discharge papers, photographs, utensils, ornaments, something from the old country, something from long ago. Experiences become validated, and children become more notable and intelligible to themselves and to others (including us); stronger, more able.

I tell students that I'll teach them "interviewing techniques," and then I show them how to use a tape recorder and how to plan an interview. I set them to interviewing each other for practice with questions like: What is the best thing about school? What do you want to do in class that you never get to do? This can lead to wonderful flights of fancy—"I never get to skydive"—or to insights about particular kids, or gaps in my own teaching—"I never get to build with wood here"; "We don't go outside enough."

When teachers value their children's opinions and experiences, children begin to think more openly, and we begin to see them differently. Later we will move to interviewing other children in the school, parents, brothers and sisters, grandparents, neighbors, community residents. We might develop a research project of general interest, and interviewing will take on new importance.

I like developing a treasure hunt with children based on what I know, and on what seems worthwhile for me and others to know. In this treasure hunt, we are searching for people, not things: Find someone whose mom sings in a choir; find someone who has a disabled family member and find out something the family learned from this experience; find someone who has an old person living at home and find out what the best part of that experience is. This kind of activity, too, can affirm the learner, and can make each child more whole, more recognizable and well-defined, more fully present in the classroom.

I have almost always begun the year by asking students to think about their own learning agendas: What do you want to do this year? What do you hope to get out of it? What is kindergarten or eighth grade going to be like? Young children are quick to answer: I'm going to play with my friends; I want to learn to spell; Mom says I'm going to learn to read! These responses help me focus—I must remember the importance of play and friendship, but also the expectation of becoming a more competent speller. Older kids have been in school too long and their answers come more slowly. "What do you want me to do?"—this is the response of the "good" student. Others might say that they just want to survive another year. Seriously pursuing a child's goals in school can, nonetheless, be a helpful guide to teaching.

The point in all of this is to create a range of ways for children to tell us about themselves, to become more whole and more fully alive in the classroom. No single activity will be powerful for everyone; no single idea will tell the whole of it. But by letting the child's school work become an aid in the teacher's investigation of children, everyone benefits. The school experience can then become stronger and deeper.

A useful approach to child observation was developed at Prospect School in North Bennington, Vermont. Pat Carini and her colleagues created an impressive archive and research center where they have collected the work of hundreds of children over many years. They have documented the school lives of children, and they have also created a compelling method of gathering information and creating rich, detailed portraits of individual children. Because the purpose of the Prospect approach is to develop a thick description of the complex choreography of learning—to really see the whole child as fully as possible in order to sustain and deepen the school experience for that child—there is an effort to make descriptions specific, concrete, and particular, and to avoid generalizations, conclusions, and jargon of any kind. The goal is to build on a child's strengths, abilities, and interests, and to support the teacher's efforts to create a classroom culture and structure that can better nurture and challenge the particular learner. The observation, recording, presentation, and recommendations at Prospect are assumed to be dynamic, changing, and in the service of an ongoing teacher inquiry: Given all the knowledge and information I now have, how shall I teach this student?

The approach at Prospect centers around a "staff review" of a child. This requires a group of teachers working together, optimally in the same school, but sometimes in a support group of teachers from several schools. The staff review contributes to teacher growth and development by creating a formal and regular focus on children. It helps us keep our attention on our shared interest and commitment. We learn a lot about one another when we talk together about children. We build colleagueship and support around the central purpose of our professional lives—student learning. Staff review allows teachers to become more critical, more invested, and more intellectually alive to the complexity of teaching. Staff review can be seen as a child-centered approach to staff development.

The staff review requires a teacher to gather together work samples, anecdotal records, observational data, impressions, and artifacts of a student, and to develop an initial "presenting" description. The teacher attempts to describe the child through multiple perspectives, including: the child's physical presence, stance in the world, gestures, posture, and energy; the child's temperament, disposition, affect, expressiveness, emotional range, and intensity; the child's attachments, commitments, and relationships with other children and adults; the child's interests, and involvement in activities; the child's modes of approach and interest in formal learning; and the child's areas of greatest strength and greatest vulnerability. Wrestling with these areas, attempting to uncover and present something meaningful about each, is a beginning.

Here is how David Carroll and Pat Carini (1989) present a youngster at Prospect:

> Sid (a pseudonym) is a tall, long-limbed nine year old with an insistent voice and noticeably awkward movements. When he first entered the Prospect School as an eight year old, his tendency to spread out, oblivious of both body and belongings, frequently irritated his fellow students. He bumped into them, jarred them with loud noises, or disturbed their work. His lack of self awareness put people off. Although he slowly gained a place among the other children, it took considerable mediating on the part of his teacher for him to gain acceptance from the group. Sid's responses were puzzling. His initial reaction to the conflict his behavior provoked was often panic and denial. Efforts to encourage greater self-consciousness and responsibility met with meager success.
>
> Yet, his face would light up with wonder when an idea caught his interest. His full attention was captured by anything mysterious, a problem requiring analysis, or connections to be found among an array of elements. An avid if careless reader, he was full of information, and he liked the attention of adults. A student teacher working in the classroom at the time described Sid's reading: "Sid . . . is often so carried away in the sound and expression of the words that his ability to clarify and comprehend are neglected without someone there to slow him down and mediate between the text and its meaning. But he seems to enjoy as well as benefit from reading aloud . . . letting all that feeling come out while having the opportunity to go back over specific words and action. I think he likes the audience too." (p. 4)

The teacher attempts to focus the staff review on some central issue or problem around which she is seeking support or recommendations. She identifies areas of confusion or uncertainty in teaching this child. In this case, it was noted that:

> [Jessica Howard, Sid's teacher] described Sid as ordinarily expressive and lively when talking about ideas and information, but noted that when situations called for a statement of value or feeling, such as settling a

social conflict, Sid's attitude of puzzlement, his flat tone, and his urgency to conclude tended to hinder conversation or stop it altogether. She added her strong impression that Sid found these occasions as frustrating and unsatisfactory as she and his classmates did. . . . She also brought to the group's attention a notable exception to his loss of expression around feeling—one that later proved to increase her understanding of Sid. She reported that in drama Sid is animated and graceful, displaying a real talent for clever improvisation and embellishment. His sense of timing, pace, expression, and imagery are "on the mark" from the first rehearsal, suggesting an ability to grasp easily the tone and overall idea of plot.

She went on to list Sid's preferred activities in the classroom: drawing and storytelling with others, cooking, designing marble chutes and mazes with blocks, making small plasticene figures for dramatic play, and building intricate constructions. . . .

Jessica described Sid's progress in reading, writing, math, social studies, and science. In all areas she emphasized his breadth of understanding and inattention to detail. His writing is fluent, to the point, and expressive of his own opinions, but marred by enormously untidy handwriting.

Jessica illustrated Sid's broad understanding with an example from math. Sid often creates his own processes for solving certain computation problems: In order to add 27 and 8, Sid would say, "Well, add 3 to the 7, that makes 30 . . . so, 35." His approach frequently leaves implicit such steps as the compensation of subtracting 3 from 8 in the example given. These "details" can trip Sid up unless someone recognizes his unconventional procedure and explains to him how his invented approach fits in the number system. Jessica noted Sid's pleasure in these explanations and that he puts them to good use.

In reading, Sid prefers a book such as The Hobbit that offers him a whole world to explore and a landscape made for heroic adventure. She confirmed the student teacher's observation that the pace of Sid's mental travel is rapid and his attention mainly focused on the action. Covering the terrain in giant steps, he often overlooks key details because he is so absorbed in the unfolding drama. He is grateful for the adult support in sorting out the story. (pp. 4–5)

Typically, another teacher, designated the chair for this review, summarizes the presentation and offers any available historical perspectives or records. Other teachers who know or who work with the child are then invited to offer specific additional information.

Questions and comments from all participants extend the presentation. If any colleagues have made formal observations of the child, these are presented and discussed. Again the chair summarizes, and now invites recommendations for the consideration of the presenting teacher. Recommendations may start out as broad and open, but will move over time toward a workable action plan. The review of Sid led to this:

> Participants affirmed Jessica's willingness to trace the perimeters of social situations for Sid, and suggested that this approach be used more intentionally and consistently. Even using the vocabulary of "mapping out" in these situations might usefully connect her efforts with Sid's own talents for internal mapping of a large picture or context. The group suggested that mapping itself may indeed be an apt metaphor for one of Sid's most reliable and preferred ways of knowing and learning. Since mapping is a way of forming knowledge across disciplines in timelines, scientific classification, and mathematical patterns, Sid might be encouraged in these directions.
>
> To expand the repertoire of classroom dramatic activities so useful to Sid, the group recommended choral reading, radio plays based on books, and lip synching to popular music. To increase Sid's access to expressed, but bounded, feeling and imagery, the group recommended more deliberate engagement with poetry and music. The group stressed that Sid needs time and occasions to find and make his own connections. A classroom with adults available to mediate his daily social contact with others is already an invaluable support to him.
>
> Most importantly, this Staff Review shifted the focus from Sid's awkward social relations, gaps in language, and mounting frustration to his strengths: skill in large scale thought, pleasure in problem solving pursuits, and intuitive vision. To undergo a formal process which allows a teacher to see a child's strengths much more clearly is a transforming experience.
>
> Jessica's year-end report to Sid and his parents reflects the benefits to both Sid and herself of the insights gained in the Staff Review:
>
> "Sid's term has been predictably full and productive for him. He continues to invest in his projects with energy and enthusiasm. His relationship to the group has stabilized, though Sid still has ups and downs in his capacity to be careful of and more attentive to who and what is around him. . . . There is a general ease in addressing Sid, and an appreciation of his capacity to be helpful in group projects and to generate good ideas. Sid himself is less self-excusing about difficult incidents, though his pattern continues somewhat. He is more articulate and outspoken about how he is feeling, and certainly more aware after the fact of how he contributed to the difficulties. On the whole, Sid has a good, steady, visible place in the group and a variety of associates to choose from for his activities." (pp. 7–8)

The session ends with a critical discussion of the process, and a formal reminder of the importance of safeguarding the privacy of the child and family. Staff review is one way to take seriously teachers' hard-won, personal knowledge of children, to reflect on it sincerely, and to make it available and public. It provides the opportunity for teachers to think more deeply about the heart of their work. And it works against stereotypes and simple explanations of any type.

Pat Carini (1979) argues that "each person is and remains an ultimate mystery" (p. 4). She has in mind both the complexity of the human experience—the contradictions, oppositions, and dazzling array of patterns and themes that mark each human life—and the ways each life embodies humanity's universal quests. She reminds us that each person mirrors all people, and that each is also a unique and specific expression of life's longing for itself. She draws our attention to the depth and complexity of each life, the dynamic nature of a life being lived—always in construction, forever part of the matrix of a larger humanity.

Carini helps us to recognize that when we observe persons, we are both the seer and the seen, and that seeing ourselves seeing—being aware of the unity embodied in our observations—is critical if we are to avoid blindness and "profane vision," the reduction of the observed into objects for use. "The person can be illuminated," she says, but "finally, the person is never fully disclosed" (p. 8). This is as true for others as for ourselves—there is simply no single dimension that tells all there is to know about any of us. Staying open to mystery, to the recognition that there is always more to know and more to be, is to allow students their full humanity, and to stay alive as a teacher.

3

CREATING AN ENVIRONMENT FOR LEARNING

A large part of the work of teaching is constructing the laboratory for learning: It must be sufficiently broad and varied to challenge a range of interests and abilities, and yet focused enough to offer students some coherent rhythms and goals. The learning environment is a complex, living reflection of a teacher's values.

When you walk into some people's spaces, you are embraced with an identifiable feeling. Harriet and Efrem's house always fills me with tranquility—to get there I have to follow a stone path that winds past a gate and through night lilies and mimosas and hibiscus, and so I feel that I'm discovering a little cottage in the woods rather than returning to a big-city basement flat. Inside, everything is neat and serene: surfaces are wood and tile, jars are filled with herbs and spices, I sleep on a cotton mat covered with a richly-colored print under a beautiful canopy. Paintings, masks, prints, sketches are arranged subtly on walls and shelves and they evoke Asian images. The bathroom is filled with ferns, and the extra-large tub is sunk into a wood frame surrounded by oils and bath salts. The space is calm; it would be difficult even for me to be loud or speedy here. I am touched with a sense of peacefulness and healing.

BJ's apartment honors the work and intentions of young children. Tiny furniture is everywhere, including a table and sofa, make-believe sink and kitchen, adorable little rocking chairs. There is a climbing frame, two easels, a shelf of blocks, and a cozy reading corner with lots of books and pillows. A large cardboard packing box has been cut into a perfect play-house for three-year-olds, and the walls are dominated by children's art. Every light switch has a clever extension so that a young child can control it, and a little half-refrigerator sits near the floor where juice and fruit and yogurt are easily available. A child-proof fence encircles the stove in the kitchen, while a moveable three-step staircase provides easy access to the sink or toilet in the bathroom. This is a place where preschoolers can be safe and yet powerful—it is an inviting, enabling space for "threes." At BJ's, the message is: Be a kid!

Coretta's house speaks of efficiency, utility, and the importance of Jesus in her life. She lives here with her husband, several grown children, and many grandchildren, and she is always prepared to feed a crowd. Everything is clean—polished and gleaming—and the invocation to remove your shoes is a stark and symbolic reminder to leave the city streets behind. One small room in the basement is finished with wood-paneling and designed as a chapel: small pews pushed close together, an altar in the front, hymnals and Bibles everywhere. Coretta's house invites you to pray.

Finally, Malcolm and Sue's house is dominated by the kitchen: It is the physical and social center, and it flows naturally into every other space. Well-thumbed cookbooks, stained with spills and layered with penciled notes from generations of users, can be found in every room. Black cast-iron pots and skillets hang from hooks, and bins of flour and dried beans line the walls. A huge, sturdy table is home to canning and baking projects, card games, hearty meals, and political meetings. Something is always cooking at Malcolm and Sue's, bubbling on the stove, baking in the oven, or "cooking" in the social activism of their community. A large screen door swings open into the garden and the boundary between outside and inside is further blurred by the fresh-cut flowers, the dried bouquets and garlic braids hanging everywhere, the bushels of plums and tomatoes, the baskets of onions waiting here and there. I love to eat and visit at Malcolm and Sue's.

All of these homes begin with a physical area that is merely given. The raw space is a shell, determined, simply there. What happens next is active choice—life is breathed into these settings by people who have certain ideas in mind, specific beliefs to enclose. And that's what makes each more than background, more than floor and walls and ceiling. That's what makes each a whole ecology of intention—the embodiment of thought and value.

All human environments have some idea, some belief worked up in them, responsibly and self-consciously or not. Some people set out with specific ideas to create particular environments. But it works the other way as well: We can look at a space and deduce ideas and beliefs from it. The space is a visible container of human action: at times oppressive or liberating; beautiful or ugly.

Environments tell us what to do. When I began teaching I used to take groups of kindergarteners to the airport to watch the planes take off and land. Now the concourse in any airport has a powerful message for all of us: move this way, keep moving, move rapidly. But to a five-year-old the concourse says, "Run!" It took me three trips to realize that my instruction—stick together, hold hands, don't run—was trumped by the environment. I was literally over-ruled by the dominant environmental voice: RUN!

What does your environment say? How could it be improved like schools?

The most taken-for-granted, sanctified, commonsense and commonplace features of life in school carry messages about important issues: this is how people learn; this is how people think; this is the nature of knowledge; this is what is valuable; this is what you should attend to. And these messages constitute a major part of what is learned and what becomes assumed about school. Why do children change grades each year? Why is the day divided into periods? Why are math and science separate subjects? Why are the children lining up in the hallway? Why is the teacher standing in front of the class doing most of the talking, and why are the students sitting at their desks most of the time, mostly quietly? The more aware we are of our thoughts and goals, the more responsible we are for our values and beliefs, the more intentional we can be in creating spaces that speak and work for us.

Students tell us their experiences of the environments we create in provocative ways: I saw a twelve-year-old friend recently dragging himself slowly along the hallway looking defeated. "Where are you headed?" I asked. "Reading," he replied glumly. "But," I said, "you love reading"—he was carrying two magazines, several comics, and a dog-eared book. "Yea," he said, "but not reading reading." School reading, reading as a mechanical matter, held no allure, even though he clearly enjoyed reading for other purposes. School had somehow turned things upside-down.

Kids understand that school is about crowds—there is no privacy and there is little individuality. What's good for the group had better be good for me. The schedule is in charge: There is a time to eat and a time to go to the bathroom, and we all go together. The intercom arbitrarily crackles on and whatever we're up to becomes unimportant—it is essential that we all hear about the double-parked car or the changed bus schedule right now. In school, authority is established, and learning about hierarchy becomes crucial; democracy is talked about but not practiced, issues of larger community interest are rarely considered and never acted on. In school, a high value is placed on quiet: "Is everything quiet?" the superintendent asks the principal, and the principal the teacher, and the teacher the child. If everything is quiet, it is assumed that all is well. This is why many normal children—considering what kind of intelligence is expected and what will be rewarded here—become passive, quiet, obedient, dull. The environment practically demands it.

Kids see that in school, learning is linked to age more than anything else, and that growth, development, and wisdom are neatly divided into nine-month units. They figure out that knowledge is cut up into disciplines, disciplines into subjects, and subjects into units of study. The day is broken into short periods, even in the early grades, and each period is devoted to a specific subject. By the fifth or sixth grade, they are typically traveling from class to class every forty or fifty minutes to be taught by a subject-matter specialist, presumably a mathematician, a scientist, a writer or a scholar of literature. Bells ring, science books are put away, people move about, and math books come out. Kids discover that adults see learning as bit-by-bit, every bit lined up as in a series—after two hundred days of schooling, each student will have added two hundred bits of math, two hundred pieces of science, two hundred slices of literature, and so on. Successful students learn to line it up.

Questioning everything in the environment, from the bottom up, is an important task for teachers. We cannot necessarily change it all but we can certainly become aware of the messages, the hidden as well as the obvious, the commonplace as well as the gaudy. We can peel the cover back a bit, peek underground, disclose the undisclosed—at least for ourselves. And in telling what is untold, we can become stronger in shaping our own environments, until they become places that more fully reflect what we know and value. We can encircle what we know about learning, embody what we value about wisdom, comprise an ecology of learning. We can become better at creating what we intend for ourselves and for our students. If I am aiming to create a classroom where kids are eager to be, where they hate to leave, where I have to finally whisk them out the door, what would I do? If I want to build a community of learners, a space kids would sometimes find more interesting than the playground, or the basketball court, or the street, how would I proceed? What would it look like? How would it be designed? What would its boundaries and its possibilities be?

A child running into my preschool classroom would see a huge collection of wooden blocks organized in a large, fenced loft space accessible up a ladder through a small hole, or along a stairway in the corner. She would be invited to build. Under the loft she would discover a dress-up area stocked with materials and "prop boxes"—milk cartons where children pull out specific items to create a make-believe hospital, pizza restaurant, shoe store, bakery, fire house, and so on. The dress-up area would feel cozy and home-like, hidden and impenetrable; a place to explore and experiment. If she wanted to work in another area, she could find paints, clay, water, sand, and art materials set up and available in a corner near the sinks. She could use something from the large collage table on wheels in one corner—a series of bins containing bits of cloth, shells, buttons, bottle caps, and corks, with small trays for getting what is needed and transporting it to the tables. Other youngsters would likely be involved with games, table blocks, dominoes, checkers, chess, and manipulative materials taken from the open cubbies close to the table and within easy reach. I want this space to say, "explore!", "experiment!"

In a classroom for older kids, I arrange three computers in one corner next to a large working loom where weaving is regularly going on; pin-hole cameras share a shelf with home video equipment. The walls are decorated with images of women in non-traditional roles, children in interesting or unique situations, African-American and Third World people engaged in productive work or interesting play. A large corner defined by a big couch, easy chairs, and a patch of carpet serves as a library where youngsters can find a range of reference books, as well as a good collection of children's literature. We have a convection oven, a small refrigerator, and a hot plate on one counter for regular snack-making and other cooking projects. On the chalk board, I have copied a series of questions that are becoming focal for this group: How do we know what we know? What is the evidence? How has it changed over time? How does it connect to other things? What difference does it make? The questions are surrounded by a thick chalk boarder with the word "SAVE" printed next to it. I want the messages to be about respect, curiosity, and critical, reflective habits of mind.

In a classroom in the detention center, we play classical music tapes on the boom box during work time, and then allow the kids to put on rap during breaks. We have a set of weights in an ante-room so the students can lift—something they love doing—during choice time, and we also have clay and a potter's wheel, a small kiln, and lots of art supplies and tools. Student projects dominate the window sills and countertops. All students have a box of books that they take to a classroom down the hall when they become "reading buddies" to a group of "shorties." Also in the box is a list of literacy activities to do with the younger kids, and forms to evaluate the reading progress of the buddy, as well as their own work as mentors. I want this room to call out to students' creativity, adolescent energy, social responsibility, and goodness.

In my classrooms, from preschool to graduate school, the work of students always adorns the walls. Stories and essays, charts and surveys, big projects and little projects are always in sight. In kindergarten, I cut outlines of each child's body from butcher block paper and ask them to paint and decorate their own images before suspending them from the ceiling. I ask college students to create reflections of themselves as teachers using construction paper, paint, clay, and found materials—these, too, go on the walls. I like children's art and I think it brings a space to life. I also like the less spontaneous, more self-conscious efforts of adult learners. In either case, students see themselves reflected in my classrooms. They see their ideas helping to shape the environment, and they see that it is my job—but not mine alone—to design the space. They see their work publicly displayed and valued. And they become more present and more visible to me and to one another through the acknowledgment of the products of their thoughts and labor.

In this one small environmental choice—the choice to display student work—I am expressing larger purposes and more overarching values: I am encouraging students to control and shape a part of their lives; I am creating a larger audience for their efforts; I am attempting to reduce the distinction between school knowledge and personal knowledge; and I am bringing their initiatives, and their personhood, into sharper focus. In this choice, I am enacting locally a range of things I believe in globally.

As a teacher, I have tried to create learning environments that suit my own larger purposes and core values. I assume, for example, that children will learn important things without a lot of well-meaning intervention. Babies will babble and eventually speak words and then sentences; they will scoot and crawl and then walk. Adults can provide safe places for them to explore and practice; we can support their efforts—sometimes crawling alongside, often babbling back, or interpreting their babble and responding appropriately, and always delighting in their accomplishments. While practically all children make these giant leaps and discoveries, we treat each one as important in its own right, unique and amazing. We don't say, "Sure, sure, everyone can walk and talk. I've seen it all before. Big deal." We don't bring in "learning specialists" to develop a curriculum unit, behavioral objectives, a scope and sequence chart, and a bunch of lesson plans (although there is, amazingly, pressure in this direction). In short, we don't do to learning to walk or to talk what we have already done to learning to read—and if we ever do, we will likely create as many nonspeakers as we have non-readers.

When each of our children learned to walk, talk, swim, ride a bike, read, or add, it was the one and only first time he would ever learn those things. The event demanded our honor and awe. And that awe was easy for us, because we knew that the learning, the effort, and the accomplishment was theirs. We had avoided—knowing that it would be irrelevant—lectures on principles of gyroscopes or the biology of fish. We supported and pushed, held on and let go, practiced swimming until we were water-logged, or bicycling until our backs ached. We provided the environment for learning and the invitation to learn. But it was their choice, their action, and their courage that resulted in the thing learned.

All real learning requires activity on some level. When our son Malik began to speak, his first word was "ball." He loved running across the kitchen floor chasing tennis balls or ping pong balls or marbles: "Ball! Ball! Ball!"

When he was three, he began to hit a whiffle ball outside with a little plastic bat. In the city, he would play wall ball for hours on end; when we visited the country, he would stand in the yard, self-pitching, and whack the ball over the house. He'd let out a whoop whenever he "roofed it."

Malik was completely satisfied to play ball—with friends or brothers when that could be arranged, or all by himself if that was necessary. There was something inherent in playing ball that held him.

As he grew and his skills developed, he learned more and more about baseball. He began to collect baseball cards and soon had a world-class collection that he would sort and re-sort in seemingly endless new organizational schemes. He memorized batting averages and he learned the lore and mythology of the game. He listened to games on the radio, went to the field when possible, and could recount heroic moments. He longed to play little league.

When he was in preschool, he asked José Vega, an assistant teacher, to play ball with him. José pitched a couple of balls and Malik "roofed" each one. Impressed, José began to pitch to Malik every day, and they developed a deep, satisfying friendship that centered around the game and continued for several years. When Malik was finally old enough to play in an organized league, his reputation was found to match his skills. The scouting report noted: "good speed, coordination, power to all fields, serious."

The point of all this is that learning requires assent and action. Learning requires practice, correction, self-correction. Learning is sometimes hard work, but if that work ties in with a sense of purpose, it can be deeply satisfying. *Learning for purpose, motivation*

I reject the idea that learning is passive, that the teacher is the "one who knows," and the students the "ones who don't know." My classroom, then, never looks like a mini-lecture hall, with an imposing teacher's desk in front and rows of students facing forward. In my room, I use the same desk—a table, really—that students use, and the "teacher's desk," a hefty oak job, is pushed to one corner where it serves as storage area and work space.

I want to build spaces that are laboratories for discovery and surprise. In an early childhood classroom of mine, this meant having a large, open area for block building and an ample set of wooden unit-blocks. The block area was surrounded by materials that suggested dramatic play with blocks—little people, animals, signs. The block shelves were adorned with magazine pictures of skyscrapers, shantytowns, and row houses, and the walls were covered with photographs of block projects gone by.

In this classroom, I made several easels, and there were canisters of red, yellow, and blue paint available. Paper was stacked nearby so that children could take a piece and snap it easily into place. There was a convenient drying rack, and children's paintings hung around the painting area.

Some educators would say that blocks and painting are for preschoolers, that they are fine for play but that by kindergarten or first grade, they must make way for "real work," meaning some form of skill and drill. Perhaps these teachers have never explored the materials adequately enough to understand the potential and power in paint and blocks, or have never seen the astonishment on the face of a six-year-old who invents the wheel for his truck, a seven-year-old who figures out how to get cars up on her massive, two-tiered bridge, or an eight-year-old who recreates Central Park and essentially retraces the landscape architect's dilemmas regarding multiple and contradictory use. Perhaps they have never witnessed the discovery of purple—a discovery that is as common as mud when children play at the easel in this type of environment, and yet dazzling in its particulars every time.

Eleanor Duckworth (1987), an amazing teacher and an intrepid investigator of children's learning, argues that the essence of cognitive development at any age is "the having of wonderful ideas" (p. 1). She has in mind the importance of discovery and surprise in all intellectual growth. For Duckworth, the discovery of purple is not trivial but profound: It provides the basis, in an amazing and memorable encounter, for constructing deep knowledge about primary and secondary colors. Along with the color purple comes confidence, self-esteem, curiosity, and a sense that knowledge is open-ended, and that knowing is active. The learner feels strengthened, energized, powerful in the world, and the lesson is deeply embedded in his or her consciousness. It is more efficient, perhaps, to teach primary and secondary colors using a work sheet and a sequence of lessons delivered by the teacher. The problem is that the collateral lessons in this more anemic approach include a sense that knowledge is finite and knowing passive, that teachers "know" and students "don't know," that somehow the important stuff will all be brought to you in order and on time—absolutely disastrous lessons if curious and critical dispositions of mind is a goal.

In classrooms for older children, blocks give way to other materials and activities but the challenge remains the same: to create laboratories for discovery and surprise, spaces where children can be active and experimental in following their own compelling goals, places where knowledge opens into future knowledge. Children in all classrooms need a project (or several projects) to pursue during some part of each day. Projects can integrate and give meaning to other aspects of school and the curriculum; projects can engage and focus children's energy; projects can be phenomenally economical, doing double duty, triple duty, quadruple duty in fulfilling linear mandates and impoverished guidelines. In a classroom for ten-year-olds, where block building was a recent memory, I worked with children to build a space station out of Leggos, and later a city out of balsa wood and glue. When the problem of bridging a highway and then a river presented itself, I issued a challenge: Using toothpicks, glue, and twine, small groups constructed the strongest possible bridges of a given height

("This boat must fit under the bridge "), and established space ("And the bridge has to connect this street to that shore."). Once the bridges were designed and built, and the process recorded in diagrams, written descriptions, and on film, the bridges were tested for maximum strength by adding small weights to them until each collapsed. Along the way, there was a lot of hypothesizing, predicting, observing, drafting, speculating, hilarity, and open-ended discussion. There were journeys to nearby bridges, and bridge photographs clipped from newspapers and magazines. Trips to the library, research, sketches, and architectural investigation followed. There was ongoing talk of bridge safety and bridge repair, suspension bridges, and trestles and viaducts. We read about the history of bridges, bridges in art, *Three Billy Goats Gruff, The Bridge Over the River Kwai, For Whom the Bell Tolls,* and more. Artfully done, bridges (like most anything) can open up the whole world, and they can never be completely finished. I suggested a culminating project—"Let's build a bridge we can actually walk across from the chess boards to the computer area, constructed with two-by-fours, one by twos, nails, and clothesline"—but I never suggested that we had "covered" bridges. No such thing. If you keep going, you can get a Ph.D. in bridges—bridge design, bridge engineering, bridge history.

In a classroom for twelve-year-olds, we were challenged one winter morning by the sighting of a snowy owl nesting near a Chicago steel plant, far south of what one would imagine its territory to be, and an inappropriate urban space for such a mythic creature. A project emerged: We wanted to figure out where it came from, how it got there, and how it was living. We searched for owl pellets (yuk), interviewed naturalists (wow), headed back to the library. We put out a simple newsletter for the school called "The Snowy Owl Investigator." We pulled out a sextant and star charts to pursue navigation, and we mapped all of North America in search of its path here and its way home.

In all of this, the goal was to make the classroom environment a learning laboratory, an active workshop for discovery. I wanted to challenge youngsters to pursue their work, their interests, their knowledge. I wanted to demonstrate to them that they were capable and potentially strong in that pursuit, that knowledge was available to them and was not some fixed entity locked up in textbooks, and that learning can be exciting, potentially awesome, and deeply satisfying. I also wanted them to read, write, figure, and so on, but my larger purpose demanded that I teach reading, for example, in the service of discovery and becoming powerful; that I resist reducing mathematics *classroom familiar but also diff than what used to.*

to a purely technical skill. Reading, math, science, geography, history—all of these were attended to seriously, but always in light of larger goals and purposes.

I want to build spaces where each person is visible to me and to everyone else, where students are known and understood, where they feel safe and valued. I want the context of students' lives to provide a lot of the raw material for learning, and I want there to be an easy flow between their worlds—an interactive, porous, integrated, and relational environment for living and learning. In other words, I want their home and community lives to impact the classroom in positive and apparent ways, and I want the classroom to influence their larger arenas of living as well. I want every youngster to have a respected private space in the room, and I want everyone to find something familiar, as well as something interestingly strange there.

In my space, there must be a wide range of ways to succeed, multiple interests to pursue, a variety of possible contributions to make. This means the room is decentralized and characterized by lively work stations or interest areas, rather than by straight rows. In an early childhood classroom of mine, there was a block area, an art space, a sand and water table, a library or reading corner, shelves for manipulative materials like rods and cubes, and a dress-up or dramatic play area. Remember? In a middle-years classroom, the space shifts somewhat: The block area gives way to a wood-working space, the sand table to a diorama in construction, the math manipulatives to more sophisticated puzzles and board games, and the dress-up corner to a fantasy adventure area. In an adolescent classroom, there are other changes: a game center featuring chess, go, and backgammon; a mapping space with cartographers' tools and surveying equipment; an architectural center; and a photography lab.

Every area, of course, serves multiple purposes. The early childhood dress-up area allows children to experience, talk through, and recreate in play important issues in their lives, but it can also be a place that is rich in written language and beginning math concepts. Teachers thoughtfully label parts of the area, and props are available (pizza boxes and pizza rounds cut into eight pieces, stethoscopes, elastic bandages) that suggest counting, organizing, correspondence, and interrelation. Similarly, the photography lab is related to visual arts, but it also intentionally involves chemistry, physics, math, and reading.

The point here is to broaden the range of skills, interests, talents, and intelligences that are stimulated and developed in this space. Rather than narrowing to the most meager, easiest-to-test strand of cognition and calling that intelligence, I want my space to say, "Intelligence is broad, open, and sparkling—whatever intelligence you bring can find a home as well as a challenge here."

My space has lots of books—lots and lots and lots of books. I want students to read a wide range of materials for a variety of purposes—for information, entertainment, adventure, knowledge, fun, wisdom, perspective, growth. I want them to see themselves in books and to see, as well, worlds that are dazzling in their diversity. I want them to find people—women as well as men, African-American and Third World people as well as whites and Europeans—acting intelligently and compassionately, solving problems, overcoming obstacles, and helping one another.

I have always had a research area where students can find dictionaries, encyclopedias, almanacs, atlases, and a wonderful, eclectic collection of weird and classic reference books—*Birds of Africa, Folksongs of the Catskills, Gray's Anatomy, The Complete Book of Canning, A Fisherman's Guide to Fly-Tying,* and on and on. This accounts for a common refrain heard in my space: "Look it up."

I have always had a closet bursting with stuff we might need in order to extend or support our work: cloth, needles and thread, all manner of found and scrounged materials (buttons, bits of plastic, rubber tubing), magazines, newspapers, cameras, tape recorders, computer paper, yarn, wood, clay, cardboard, and more. I have a computer, a small potter's wheel, a little loom, and a silk-screen frame. Not everything is in use all the time, of course, but day to day, year to year nothing is thrown away, either. Another common refrain: "Let's see if we can find something in the closet for that."

My space has always had plants to care for—big, hearty survivors as well as little seedlings we are coaxing to life—and animals to look after; fish, gerbils, turtles, a rabbit. Plants and animals can help to set a caring and responsible tone in a classroom. They can also provoke thought and questions that lead to careful observation and record-keeping—they can lead a class in a hundred different useful directions if they are an integral part of the learning environment.

In my classrooms—preschool through high school— something was always cooking. Cooking is a class job, a responsibility, and so four or five people cook every day. In the beginning, we were cooking without heat—"cool cooking." There were a lot of fruit salads, peanut butter play-dough, coconut balls, and celery boats. Later, I learned how to make an oven using a cardboard box with a tight-fitting lid, tin-foil, wire hangers, light bulbs, and sockets. Making the oven was interesting in its own right—it took days and days—and our ovens successfully baked granola, pies, and quick-baked breads. Of course, when I got a hot plate, a toaster oven, and then a microwave, we cooked to make money for special projects, and we baked to celebrate special events. We became world-class. I didn't want any kid graduating from my class who couldn't bake a cake, a pie, and a loaf of bread, or make one main dish: roti, tortillas, pasta putenesca, pizza, farm tofu. Cooking is engaging for lots of children, and it is an area into which they can bring their own knowledge and skill, as well as deepen and develop their understanding. When a teacher carefully creates the time and space to cook, she can thoughtfully build in reading, math, science, history, culture, mapping, and more.

Bringing together several of my core beliefs about learning and the purposes of schooling will help me shape an even more appropriate classroom environment. For example:

- I believe that people create and construct knowledge, and that learning is an active process that requires energy and assent. Learning involves physical and mental interaction with things and ideas, and it is most often characterized by discovery and surprise.
- I believe that human development is complex and interactive, and that it is not useful to separate physical, emotional, social, and intellectual growth. We are all whole people—cognition is entwined with affect, and my mind (and yours) is embedded in spiritual, cultural, and psychological being.
- I believe that people learn best when they are nurtured as well as challenged, when they are allowed to explore, experiment, and take risks. We learn when we feel good about ourselves and others, when we trust the environment and the people in our lives, when we are safe.
- I believe that learning is powerful when information is integrated into experiences and larger personal contexts. Discreet bits and pieces of information, random and disconnected, are not strong building blocks toward knowledge.
- I believe that culture is the frame through which all of us make sense of the world. All culture is dynamic and porous, and exploring both our collective culture and our various cultural differences can become an incredibly rich intellectual adventure at any age.

- I believe that all children can learn, and that every youngster should be afforded multiple occasions to accomplish something of value in school. The range of opportunities to experience success must be wide and not narrow.
- I believe that the purpose of school is to open doors, open worlds, and open possibilities for each person to live life fully and well. School must provide students access to all the important literacies of our place and time, and it must help them develop the dispositions of mind that will allow them to be powerful in shaping and reshaping the future. In a democracy, schools have a specific responsibility to educate for active citizenship and democratic living.
- I believe that life in school must be thought of as life itself, not simply preparation for later life. Life in school—for adults as well as for children—must be lived fully. And, again, in a democracy, school life should embody democratic (rather than say, authoritarian, autocratic, bureaucratic, or feudal) principles.
- I believe that teachers must create opportunities for learners to become more skilled, more able, more powerful. Teachers must ask themselves what is most worthwhile for people to know and experience, and what are the best ways to provide access to that knowledge and experience. Teachers must issue a compelling invitation to learn, and then become guides and mentors to learners in that immense journey.

These beliefs—these core values or basic principles—can be brought to life in thousands on thousands of ways. There is no fixed, one-to-one correspondence between a large idea or value and a specific classroom practice. I have tinkered, adjusted, struggled over big questions, and fine-tuned tiny details—and I have never been completely satisfied. The environment—like the students is a living thing. It changes every day, every hour, and it can be unpredictable, strange, idiosyncratic. Visiting my classroom in September offers one snapshot; a return visit in November will find a very different space. This laboratory is a space of ongoing experimentation for about thirty people; it is constantly being torn down and rebuilt. There is always room for growth and improvement.

Noting, for example, that "learning is characterized by discovery and surprise" does not, in itself, tell me what to do. It is not a blueprint for action. I still need to think, explore, imagine, and finally choose a course of action from a dazzling array of possibilities. But in that journey, I can hold this belief as a useful reference point, a lens to make my choices clearer. In this case I can know that some of the materials and activities and routine in my classroom should not be entirely structured, pre-specified, or one-dimensional; some should be open-ended and organized around the unforeseen, thereby inviting astonishment and wonder both from the students and from me.

Mara Sapon-Shevin (1990), an exemplary teacher, argues that one central organizing goal in our schools must be the creation of communities of care and compassion. She has in mind building classrooms that honor learners as whole people, and teachers as moral agents. The primary obligation of educators, she insists, is to assist in the realization of each student's full humanity—and this obligation may include direct instruction, but it goes way beyond conveying any specific facts or body of information to children. It includes creating environments that challenge and nurture the wide range of learners who actually appear in our classrooms, and developing spaces that embody what we take to be valuable and worthwhile. And it means structuring opportunities for cooperation, active participation, decision-making, and moral reflection.

Even though we long for community—for places of common vision, shared purpose, cooperative effort, and personal fulfillment within collective commitment—we most often settle for institutions. That is, we generally find ourselves in impersonal places characterized by interchangeable parts, hierarchy, competition, and layers of supervision. Communities have problems and possibilities; schools and universities have departments. We are too often reduced to clerks or bureaucrats in these places, and our sense of purpose and agency is diminished.

While this is a universal problem of modern life, it impacts teachers in specifically harsh and brutal ways. Teaching, if it is to be done well, must be built on vision and commitment; learning, if it is to be meaningful, depends on imagination, risk-taking, intention, and invention. Stripped of these elements, teaching is mechanical and sterile, and learning is the stuff of pigeons pecking for food or mice running a maze.

For Sapon-Shevin, the teacher is neither an autocrat nor a cipher, neither lecturer nor do-nothing. The teacher establishes the boundaries of safety, trust, truth-telling, and fidelity. She is focused on the persons before her—whole persons with bodies, minds, feelings, and spirits—and she resists thinking of teaching in terms of test scores or control. She invites youngsters to enter as whole people and to bring their skills, interests, experiences, and dreams into this collective space, and then to shape and reshape it in their own images. She will be fully present too. Her passions—singing, quilting, hiking, dancing—will be well represented. Now she is set and the drama can begin—the next step is building bridges from the known to the not-yet-known.

4

BUILDING BRIDGES

Teachers are explorers. As they explore the world and the lives of their students, they cast lines to different ways of thinking. Teaching is often bridge-building; Beginning on one shore with the knowledge, experience, know-how, and interests of the student, the teacher moves toward broader horizons and deeper ways of knowing.

When Zayd was twelve, and beginning to feel the stirrings that would transform him from childhood to adulthood, he attended his friend Bear's bar mitzvah. "It was so cool," he reported. "Bear played cello for everyone and gave a speech. And then people talked about his life and what he had done so far, and what he might do in the future." Zayd was moved by all the thought and care people had put into this ritual of passage, and he was impressed with the proclamation that Bear was now a man, a person with new responsibilities and freedoms. "You could see him stretching and growing right through the ceremony," Zayd said. "And when it was done, he looked different."

Zayd resolved to organize a ceremony for himself, some ritualistic way to mark his own coming of age. He enlisted his mother, Bernardine, as his mentor, guide, and fellow traveler. Together, they began a quest to create something special, something that would both fit Zayd's unique pathway and connect to more universal themes of passage through life. It was a large undertaking, and yet each approached the task with enthusiasm and commitment.

A conversation began in our home, and it grew over many months to embrace our extended family, friends, colleagues, acquaintances. Partly, the conversation centered around questions: What does it mean to become an adult? What are some of the changes that occur? What are the physical alterations, and what are the emotional or psychological upheavals? Which changes are additive and measurable, and which are about quality and character? Do adults think differently from children; and do they in every instance? How do you know? Can people choose to change in certain ways? Can they resist certain turns and adjustments? How much of growth is predestined? How much of who we are is determined genetically or biologically, and how much socially or culturally? Why is adolescence considered a time of upheaval and rebellion? Must it be so?

As the conversation turned and grew and developed, it became knottier, thornier, and more fun. There were always more questions: In some cultures you really are a woman or a man at age thirteen, so why not in ours? What is the difference between being "full grown" and being "adult?" Why can't I drive until I'm sixteen, vote until I'm eighteen, or drink beer until I'm twenty-one? Who decides these things? What do these events mean in terms of growing up?

One hard and troubling question emerged from the pages of the newspaper. Bernardine and Zayd read and discussed the *New York Times* coverage of the Central Park rape trial. Now they were on to the particular problems of "manhood" in our culture, and also issues of group violence, race, gender, and sex, and questions of responsibilities and rights. As they followed the trial and cultivated their conversation, they explored the difficulty of ethical choice in the context of a crowd. Does a group make you stronger, or more anonymous? Why do people act differently in groups than on their own? Why are groups particularly powerful for adolescents? Or are they? Can a group make you do something you know to be wrong? How?

Alongside the questions and ongoing conversation was a more formal inquiry into coming-of-age. Bernardine read several books aloud to Zayd and his brothers and friends. She read traditional books like *David Copperfield* and *A Tale of Two Cities*, by Charles Dickens and *Little Women*, *Little Men*, and *Jo's Boys*, by Louisa May Alcott; autobiographies like *Malcolm X*, *The Diary of Anne Frank*, and *Coming of Age in Mississippi*, by Ann Moody, ethnographies like *Coming of Age in Samoa*, by Margaret Mead, and *Seven Arrows*, by Hyemeyohsts Storm; and a hodgepodge of novels and short stories, like *Walkabout*, by James Vance Marshall, *The Red Badge of Courage*, by Stephen Crane, *Annie John*, by Jamaica Kincaid, *The Way to Rainy Mountain*, by Scot Momaday, *The Man Who Killed a Deer*, by Frank Waters, *Journey to Topaz*, by Yoshiko Uchida, and *The Education of Little Tree*, by Forrest Carter.

The reading engaged Zayd's brothers and friends and became an important tool to deepen the discussion, to ground it and extend it into different times and places and new and unheard of worlds. And the reading was always brought more intensely into focus by the approach of adulthood and the immediate question driving the whole project: How shall I mark my coming-of-age?

Zayd enjoyed the reading, the conversation, and the attention enormously. He became personally involved in each story, urgently interested in every bit of information he could co-opt to his purposes. In the work of Mari Sandoz he found a second guide. Sandoz brought the culture of the Sioux people to life for Zayd in *Those Were the Sioux, Old Jules,* and, particularly, in *Crazy Horse.* He read and reread the story of Crazy Horse, how he lived, what he accomplished, especially how he was the "Strange Man of the Oglalas," and came to be a man and then a leader among his people. Zayd was captivated, and Crazy Horse helped him create and shape the right ritual.

Several months before his thirteenth birthday, Zayd wrote himself a simple challenge:

> There are three crafts I would like to try to make in the next four months. I will try to make them as soulful and full of spirit as I possibly can. I am trying to put my life story into these three objects. They will be my medicine. These three are:
>
>   1. A ceremonial buckskin shield. This is my biggest project so I am putting the most time into it. I am going to try to make it simple but beautiful because too much detail crowds the essence of things.
>   2. A buckskin vest/shirt to wear during my vision quest. In this, like the shield, I am trying to achieve beautiful simplicity.
>   3. A coup stick. This will not be a weapon used for killing but instead my medicine, symbolizing my personal struggles and victories.

Work on these "three crafts" became an intense journey. The ceremonial shield, for example, took shape when Zayd found a perfect branch, which he and Bernardine soaked in the bathtub and slowly, slowly bent into a circle. They bought a scrap of pale buckskin at a leather goods store, stretched it to fit the frame, and then struggled to stitch it into place without any folds or distorting creases. Finally Zayd painted on its face a white buffalo skull with three streaks of red to the skull's right side. "This symbolizes blood and the careless wasting of life," he said.

Zayd attached to the frame hawk and turkey feathers he had collected, and he painted "the symbols of my life" onto the buckskin. These symbols were primitive-looking markings signifying conception, growth, childhood, adulthood, and death, and they appeared on each of his "crafts."

Zayd also gathered some poems to use in his ceremony, and he wrote two poems himself:

> 1. Do not look backward
> on the finite shadows of the past
> instead
> walk tall and proud
> into the unlimited expanse
> of the future.

> 2. SACRIFICE
> The string is pulled back
> as the bow melts into my arm
> and the target into my eyes.
> It
> and I
> become one.
> The arrow is loosed
> and the wind takes it.
> caresses it
> hands it to the bear:
> the bear gives me its meat
> and I eat it
> and because of its death
> my life goes on.

Finally, he wrote an invocation:

> A Boy
> When a boy becomes a man he takes on certain responsibilities to himself, his friends and family, and his world as a whole to keep them safe and well. In this time of great change in myself as well as the world, I think of what the ensuing years will bring, the laughter and the tears, the life and the love, and I am scared to go on, but this, again, is part of becoming a man, to face life with all its qualities and faults and to eliminate the faults and make life better for all people and animals and to transcend my own faults and elongate my qualities in the hope that once I am gone, my life will have improved others' lives and bettered the world.

Zayd decided he didn't want a party of any kind, but wanted, instead, to wear his shirt and carry his stick and shield, to go to a quiet place alone to fast and seek a vision, just like Crazy Horse had done. We found a stretch of dunes, a beach, and on his birthday he trekked off out of sight while we waited. When he returned in a few hours, he told us his vision, a vision nuanced no doubt by his reading and chosen orientation. Later he wrote down what he had said:

> First there was an empty ocean beach, and then came a fire and out of this fire stepped a man. He was tall and lean, wearing a bear claw necklace and a breach cloth. Onto this beach came a buffalo; he was all white except for his horns which were black. The man took his bow and shot the buffalo. The arrow would have missed, but the buffalo turned so that it hit him. The man ate the meat and suddenly he knew all things that animals know as well as all things that men know. The man then went back to his people and walked through the streets and the people saw him and most of them walked with him because they all wanted to get where he was going. Some people did not walk with him because they were too scared. So they never got there and there were some people who ran ahead, but they got tired too quickly and didn't get there.
>
> At last, the people got to the beach where the man had killed the buffalo. The man started singing to them and all the knowledge of the animals flowed out of him like a rainbow into the people so that they knew all these things. But the man was still sad he had killed the buffalo, so he held up a shining piece of metal and all the people started singing with him. The rainbow flowed out of them and into the metal and all of a sudden, the buffalo was there.
>
> The man was happy but he had used up too much of himself bringing back the buffalo, so he walked into the sea and lay down on the ocean floor. As the man lay there, he aged very quickly, but it was not a bad kind of aging, instead of growing weaker, he grew wiser. As the man was about to die, he saw that his people were about to kill the buffalo and reclaim the knowledge of animals, so with his last dying breath the man sang again, one last time, and again the knowledge poured from his lips and flowed into the people and they saw that they should not kill the buffalo. Seeing this, the man knew he had fulfilled his purpose and finally, he died.

We all hugged and congratulated Zayd. Now he was a man—kind of. He broke his fast with his favorite dinner, carefully selected to reflect his heritage, and we opened presents and read aloud what his grandparents, uncles, aunts, and friends had written and sent to him on the occasion of his coming of age. Bernardine wrote:

GOLDEN ARROW
For Zayd at Thirteen

straight, long and true as an arrow
you lengthen into your manhood
as I had dreamed, more person than "man,"
challenging old models by your being
but with a center, at home in your self.
with a flood of sun you arrived
in our arms, a golden child, engaged
quick to laugh, to question further,
wide-awake to the world until you drop
and sleeping deeply where you land.
you too like to make your own meaning,
drawing on books and vision, heady
and hard-headed at once
inventive and easily tradition-bound
you draw ceremony from stars and strange ones.
I think of you with carousel birthdays,
a knight of the third grade round table,
cabbage wedding at Redhawk, diving from salmon cliffs,
reading at breakfast and bath, glancing back from home plate at
    Wrigley Field, liking to cuddle.
your glory casts a sprinkledust glow,
making us eager each day to find this age the best of ages, the
    bittersweet of losing how you were
honeyed by the mystery of who you are becoming,
we cherish your unique zayd ways.

And I wrote:

I am dazzled by you, by your natural gifts, your steady growth, your unique perspectives and interpretations, your insights and un-common wisdom. Now that you are a young man, it is a good time to take stock, to reflect on what you have made of what you have been made, to choose consciously where you will go next.

When you were ten you pointed out an interesting mystery about life: these past ten years went by quickly, like a flash, you said, but the next ten seem to stretch out before me endlessly. Now that you are thirteen, is it any different? Life does that, tricks you that way, and so it is important to be a thoughtful and caring choice-maker.

Choosing is the work of life. I'm certain the project you choose will be a large one, for it will have to contain your considerable intelligence, energy, and goodness over a long time. Only a big plan will have room for you in it.

Sometimes I like to think about questions in a weird way. Sometimes I ask myself, what are three things I must do before I die? And then I figure out how to do them. Or I ask, what epitaph would I want for myself? And so I ask you: What do you need to do before you die? What would you want people to say about your life? What would they say now, and what in a few years? What would your family say, your brothers, and what would your friends say, Elena and Thai, for example, Bear and BJ and Efrem, your teachers, say Steve or John or Lisa, or more distant acquaintances like Coretta, Julie, or Herb? Asking questions this way lends a certain urgency to the discussion. It's easy to coast, to be conventionally decent by ignoring society, much harder to pay attention to life, to stay wide-awake, to choose to be moral and just and caring in an indifferent and sometimes hostile or evil world.

When we met thirteen years ago, it was love at first sight. I thought I would teach you a lot, but right from the start you taught me. Another one of life's paradoxes, I guess. You taught me about unqualified love. You taught me the art of holding on and letting go. You taught me courage and creativity. What will you teach me next?

The effect of this whole process on Zayd and on all of us was fascinating. We were creating a positive view of becoming a teenager, a sense that being a teenager was a wonderful, challenging time of life, and this ran in the face of widely-held popular notions. In our culture, of course, "adolescence" is constructed as problematic at best. Teenagers are trouble. Preadolescents are painfully aware of the conventional view, and they will often worry and wonder aloud about what's going on, and what's going to happen.

The enduring theme from popular culture is something like "I was a teenage werewolf," and the real-life variations are perfectly scripted: The sweet, young child who never did anything wrong is suddenly transformed into a snarling beast driven by animal impulses; a mutant with out-of-control hormones. The eruption of hair—

especially hair—where things had been smooth and delicate is the physical signal that the horror is about to begin: The teenager is consumed with a self-loathing that turns to rage, and everyone else had better get out of the way. Teenagers are trouble at best, and probably dangerous.

The only problem with this solid bit of common sense is that it is not true. Common sense, of course, can be more dogmatic and insistent than any religion or political ideology, and the popular wisdom on teenagers is a clear case. It is as if we are all professional wrestling fans, cheering, booing, and groaning on cue as one of the brutes seems to tear the eyeball from the other's head, and yet the whole thing, including our collective gasping, is a fraud. This is not to say that the transition from childhood to adulthood is all sweetness and light, but only to suggest that there are alternative ways of looking at this particular passage, and that we need not be total victims of someone else's B-movie plot. We can try to write our own scripts.

That's what Zayd and Bernardine did. Their script was affirming, positive, built on strengths. Bernardine was conscious of challenging convention, inventing something new, and so she stayed alive to a range of questions: What are adolescents like? What are their main needs and developmental tasks? What would constitute a successful passage through these years? What kinds of experiences will likely help youngsters at this stage of life?

She could see in Zayd and his friends a new ability to think seriously about their own thinking and the thinking of others, and a new capacity for sustained abstract reasoning. She could see, as well, intense curiousity and a persistent idealism. These were some of the strengths on which to build a bridge. She found, of course, dramatic emotional and social upheaval in them, too, as they struggled to broaden bases of affiliation beyond their families and into a wider circle of friends, and as society and "the crowd" became the focus of much concern. In the same way as they passed from baby to child ten years before, these adolescents were opening to a new sense of identity and to a new way of seeing and participating in the world. And just as before, there was turmoil and some sadness, as every "yes" required a corresponding "no." Of course, now they inhabited these huge, crashing bodies, but the challenge for the adults in their lives, as before, seemed to be to figure out how to hold on to them as young children and how to let go as they became capable of flying free.

Zayd pursued his coming-of-age ceremony with single-minded intensity. Since he doesn't invest himself this fully in everything he does, what was it that made this project so special? What attracted and held him? And did it have any value beyond indulging adolescent self-centeredness?

The answers seem obvious to me. He was drawn and committed to the project because it was concentrated on something he cared deeply about—himself, yes, and the changes he was going through; a bridge he was building, but also an idea he had spawned. The idea was not, of course, original; it had been stimulated by a friend's bar mitzvah and it was, it turned out, a common ritual. But he initiated his ceremony, he authored the script, and it had his signature on it, his fingerprints all over it—he owned it. Furthermore, as it grew, wider circles of family and friends became co-conspirators in the quest. As more people signed on and the cast grew, the audience for his efforts, though distant in space, grew as well. For all of us, and for children in particular, audience infuses any project with urgency. How will I look? How will I do? Will I trip and fall? Will they think it's wonderful? Audience is a great motivator.

The value of this effort seems clear as well. The project focused this child's considerable energy in a productive direction. It brought his preferences into full view and made his intelligence, skills, and interest evident to himself and to others. With his strengths manifest, some weaknesses were also uncovered, but they were worked on in light of something larger, more important. They were never allowed to overwhelm.

The environment supported his efforts and challenged him to go further. There was both stimulation and nurturance the whole way. There was an intimate involvement between mother and son at the moment of letting go, of leaving childhood behind, and there were feelings of both excitement and sadness. Bernardine was co-author and co-learner, discovering alongside her beloved and admired student. She didn't know it all and then convey it, inert, to him; rather, she walked down the same road and used her greater knowledge and experience to question, point out the direction, challenge, and guide. She was aware that it was he who was bridging childhood to adulthood. She was conscious of gearing the project up, bringing in reading, writing, math, and science, as well as psychology, mapping, history, and cultural studies. But she was sensitive to his lead when appropriate.

This small project is a microcosm of the values implicit in a hopeful approach to teaching: the importance of love, commitment, and ethical action; the centrality of making the student visible as a whole person; the value of creating a safe and stimulating environment for reflection. It points to the danger and the difficulty inherent in teaching as it is generally constituted—teaching as crowd control, or teaching as clerking. It also moves us toward the next crucial step: the teacher's responsibility for constructing bridges from the known to the not-yet-known.

Outstanding teaching is built on a base of knowledge about students. One obvious way to collect that knowledge is by building some part of the routine around a curriculum of "ME." Zayd's project is an example of a "ME" curriculum for twelve-year-olds.

Imagine the energy that would be released if teachers of twelve-year-olds announced at the start of the school year that sometime during the year, each youngster would have the opportunity in class to carry out a coming-of-age ceremony completely of his or her own design. The ceremony might involve special foods eaten in particular, ritualistic ways; it might involve specified tasks to be performed for the community; it might involve invocations from elders or family members. In any case, there would be time in class to work on the project, and time set aside for each to perform a ceremony. In the spring, there would be a special assembly for the whole school community, including parents, and each child would read a poem or passage that embodies his or her thoughts and feelings as each enters adulthood.

In one corner of the classroom, there might be a bookshelf devoted to books and articles pertaining to the general theme of rites-of-passage. The teacher might read a few pieces aloud: a stunning description by Ilsa Dissan of the Zulu requirement that each boy kill a lion and be circumcised in order to become a man; Alex Haley's rich account of Kunta Kinte's coming-of-age ceremony; or Issac Bashevis Singer's moving story of a bar mitzvah carried out clandestinely under Nazi occupation. Or the teacher might occasionally invite grandparents, parents, and others in to share their own recollections: a confirmation ceremony, a first communion in Mexico, a "coming out" ball for the whole town. All through the year there would be the sense of preparation, of projecting toward one special day, and, finally, the public assembly before a large audience.

There are endless variations. One sixth-grade teacher I know, whose pupils each year graduate to junior high school, asks his students in January to design and construct chairs which they will use during their graduation ceremony. In this school the graduates sit on

the stage, and their chairs are prominently displayed to make a statement. The teacher asks them to research and study chair design as
well as to think deeply about what they want their chairs to "say."
This may involve a cultural or personal statement, a social comment,
or whatever. Each year, pictures of chairs from magazines and newspapers begin to fill the walls. Each year, the variety and creativity aston-
ish: a large oak seat with brightly painted coat-of-arms, a Taino throne,
a delicate post-modern tripod made of drain tubing, a rocking chair
that works, a school-form, a pew.

In any "ME" curriculum, there is variation and open-endedness.
This allows students to face and see one another, and it allows the
teacher to behold the student. There is no specified end-point; simply
by issuing the charge and structuring the time and the focus, the
teacher and students alike are freed to experiment, to attend to questions and possibilities, to lose self-consciousness in the work at hand.
The work itself becomes valuable, and the students are free to participate without concern for who is best or worst; the teacher can find
important dimensions of each student through the work. The coming-
of-age ceremony, the chair, or whatever are points of departure for
teachers—places where a child's thinking is accessible. The work
allows a teacher to wonder: Where can I go next? How can I involve
this child in looking at the work? What's up? The point is not to judge
it "good" or "bad," but to see it as a marker from somewhere, toward
somewhere else.

In earlier grades a "ME" curriculum takes other forms. In a kindergarten class of mine, I designated one wall for photographs of children and families and for children's drawings and stories about their
families. There was a special area for the "child of the week," where
each kid's work and projects were prominently displayed for five days.
There was time and space organized around a particular child's preferences and desires, again in an attempt to highlight each child, to bring
him or her into fuller view. There was a sense of specialness inherent
in the project, and a sense also of anticipation and eagerness—a chance
to author and invent something of personal importance.

In a second-grade class of mine, we published and distributed
school-wide a monthly newsletter called "All About Us." The newsletter contained poems, short-stories, interviews with one another,
drawings, charts displaying a range of surveys we had conducted (on
favorite crackers, sneakers, jeans, radio stations), crossword puzzles,
and more. One teacher I know developed a similar project into a "radio station," with a schedule each month for other classes to visit and
listen to the program. Another teacher of young children paired with

an upper-grade class and developed an oral history project, with the older children interviewing and "taking life histories" of the younger ones, and developing an archive and a set of autobiographies for general use.

Bridge-building requires someone to lay the first plank. Schools are often structured around the notion that the child should lay the first, the second, and virtually every plank after that. This is defeating for many youngsters. It seems clear enough to me that the teacher must be the architect and the contractor who begins to build the bridge. She must know the child in order to know where to put that first plank. She must also know the world, have a broad sense of where the bridge is headed, and have confidence that she and the students together can get there. And she must stay in touch with that child as the bridge takes shape, much as Bernardine did with Zayd.

Culture is an important window into a child, an essential part of any bridge's blueprint, and effective teachers must learn to be lifelong students of culture. This is an ongoing and potentially enormously satisfying challenge. Teachers can think of themselves as explorers, researchers, and ethnographers. Their workshop is the students themselves, their families and neighborhoods, and ever wider circles embracing larger and larger communities.

Culture, of course, is more than random holidays, more than haphazard artifacts. Culture includes all the surface objects and characteristic of a people—things like food, art, clothing, music, crafts, and so on. And culture embraces, as well, all the traditions and customs people create: their rituals, games, sports, dialects, habits and ways of life. But on the deepest and most subtle level, culture also embodies a people's beliefs and values, its way of looking at the world. This might include their religion and philosophy, their shared outlook, their approaches to child rearing, love-making, mating, and relating. Culture covers it all.

We miss a lot, then, if we never look beyond the "what" of culture—the things, the objects—if we never get to the "how" and the "why." We stunt our growth with ideas of culture as curiosity, as bits of exotica that some people have while others do not. Gilbert Ryle put it succinctly: Human beings spend their lives weaving webs of significance, he said, and culture is those webs. That is, culture encompasses everything beyond the biological aspect of being human. Exploring culture is beginning a bridge to something huge and complex and wonderful. This is precisely what Zayd's ceremony opened up, for himself and for us.

Culture is not a thing, a dead bug to look at under a microscope. Culture is elusive, alive, dynamic, fluid, and changing. Depending on your age, computers were probably not part of your parents' cultural heritage, but they are definitely a part of your children's. Furthermore, there is as much range and diversity within a cultural group as there is between groups. I practically live on rice and beans, for example, but that doesn't make me Mexican; I have several Mexican-American friends who rarely eat rice and beans. Finally, virtually every culture is itself the result of different people interacting, clashing, merging, relating, giving, and taking. There is no "pure" African culture or American culture or Samoan culture. The recent discovery of an isolated people in the Philippine forest was so exciting precisely because it was so rare; and, of course, that discovery led to intense interaction, and that interaction, limited as it was, created rapid and dramatic cultural changes.

Think about yourself for a minute; think about your family, your friends, your neighbors. All the things you have in your home—the clothes, the furniture, the cooking utensils, the books, the radio or the TV, the computer—all of these are cultural artifacts. Think about what you like to eat, how close you stand to another person in conversation, your view of the proper way for children to address adults—this, too, is part of your culture. And beneath all of this are your deepest beliefs, those things that you don't have to think about because they are beyond question—the way things are. We experience our own culture from the deepest levels toward the surface, and so our own culture can be largely invisible to us. The deep structures are the origins of everything, and they exert tremendous power and give meaning to the other levels of cultural experience. When we look at another culture, however, we tend to see the surface first, and we may fail to probe toward the deeper well-springs of meaning. This, too, can cut us off, and make culture and other people invisible.

When one person's cultural common sense is another's exotic behavior, the cultural whiplash can be jarring, decentering, humorous, or tragic. For example, if a teacher's understandable approach ("A direct question requires a straight-forward response.") meets a child's good upbringing ("Don't talk back and don't speak unless specifically told to speak.") the encounter can lead to all manner of misunderstandings. This teacher, a prisoner of her cultural common sense, misinterprets the children's silent deference as dullness, while these children, bound as well by their own webs of culture, fail to see what she's up to: They lose each other across a cultural gulf. The teacher must make some sustained effort to understand, to bridge the gulf.

The cultural bridge is begun by responding sensitively to the deepest realities of children's lives. Children are simply allowed to love, respect, cherish, and retain what they bring to school—their language, for example, their perceptions, their values. This becomes the base of the bridge, the place from which lines will be cast and bridge-work extended, the conceptual touchstone for each child's education. This was the base for Zayd's project. The bridge will hang together if there is connection between teacher and child, between family and school.

Teachers must understand that even as they teach, they will also be taught; even as they help others develop, they will themselves change and grow. If a teacher is to be hopeful and optimistic in her teaching, she must take action—waiting cannot bring hope. This, of course, involves a certain amount of plunging into the unknown, listening and hearing; a certain willingness to take risks at the adult level, too. It might mean soliciting or borrowing materials and ideas from parents—records, tapes, books, magazines, games, recipes. I have often asked parents for familiar plants and fruits to use in science and math. I have recorded parents telling familiar stories or singing songs or simply chatting with me on tape. I ask them to send in photographs regularly, and "cultural artifacts" on occasions when we have transformed our room into a small museum of culture. On those occasions, the room fills up with the odd and the familiar: Bibles, a crucifix, a shovel, a mortar and pestle, a set of dominoes.

Parents can give teachers important information about child-rearing practices. Perhaps some families feel strongly that children should show respect through silence, while others expect children to look adults in the eye and engage in some back and forth. Perhaps some people feel it is essential that women work outside the home and that house-work should be shared, while others insist that women cooking and being there in the home is an expression of cultural coherence. This is important information for teachers. It allows us to transform whatever sense of certainty and cultural superiority we might bring to school into a genuine search for the history and meaning behind specific practices.

When I was first teaching kindergarten, a father came to me and said that if his son cursed or misbehaved, I had permission to hit him. I was taken aback, and I thought that this father must be a harsh person who either didn't understand how to raise children or didn't care deeply about his own son. Over the course of the year, I came to know this father well, and I turned out to be wrong on both counts. He loved his son enormously and felt, based on his own experience, that while certain misbehavior, including cursing and showing disrespect, could be written off as "boys will be boys" for many children, it would more likely be interpreted as a serious problem when the child involved was an African-American male. He argued that, given the power relationships and social realities of our time and place, his son's survival depended on conforming to certain rules of behavior. While we never fully agreed on the solution, it helped me to see the problem from within. It was me, not him, who needed to grow in understanding.

Teachers can also involve children in a study of the immediate community. There can be trips, interviews, mapping, comparing, following leads, exploring the complexity of a community's life. There can be oral histories taken and lines drawn back to Latin America, Europe, Asia, Africa. Teachers can learn languages alongside of or even from their students. Trying to learn another language reminds us how difficult daily communication is for some students, and it is a sign of respect for them as well.

Teachers should certainly study culture as a phenomenon that exists "out there"; they should read about other cultures and develop a repertoire of ways to engage students and families in a dialogue on culture. But teachers and students together can also study culture as something that exists "in here"; that is, they can critically examine larger cultural issues that impact classroom life.

For example, most schools celebrate Christmas. Questions have been raised for years about the propriety of public schools using so much time and energy to promote a holiday from a specific and dominant religious group. Schools close in late December, virtually everyone must acknowledge the power of Christmas, and yet questions persist. The response has usually been that Christmas has become a generic holiday for kids and that any opposition to this particular celebration must be the work of some modern day Scrooge. Early in my teaching, Jewish parents made me aware of Chanukah, the celebration of light, and encouraged me to find a place in my classroom for acknowledging and celebrating this holiday as well. I was given a menorah, candles, dreidels, and a lovely book by Isaac Bashevis Singer, called *The Power of Light*. So, as December approached, we talked of Christmas and Chanukah, we lit candles and sewed stockings, and I searched and searched until I found a black Santa Claus we could all visit.

The next year, I read about Kwanzaa, a nonreligious African-American cultural celebration developed in 1966 by Dr. Maulana Ron Karenga, a Black Studies professor at California State University in Los Angeles. Kwanzaa lasts from December 26 until January 1, and involves candle-lighting, artistic and musical presentations, community dinners, and wide discussion of seven principles, one of which is highlighted each day: Umoja means "unity," Kujichagulia means "self-determination," Ujima means "collective work and responsibility," Ujamaa means "cooperative economics," Nia means "purpose," Kuumba means "creativity," and Imani means "faith." Now we celebrated Kwanzaa as well as Christmas and Chanukah, and we learned to make our own candles, some ivory, others black, red, and green. Alongside the menorah stood a Kinara, a candleholder "symbolic of our roots, our parent people, Continental Africans."

Soon we discovered a traditional pagan celebration of the Winter Solstice from England, and then Three Kings Day, a celebration of the Epiphany from several Latino countries. The fast of Ramadan was a recent addition. Now we were singing a wider range of songs, dancing, reading, studying, exchanging gifts, reciting passages, hiding straw, lighting candles—and studying ourselves and others. We worked to avoid the "holiday syndrome"—the treatment of culture as curiosity, a people's story as token gesture—and we struggled to create a deep and sustained engagement with cultural study. It was a thick stew; it fed each of us and there was always more to go around. And yet the question remained: Aren't all of these add-ons simply inferior Christmases? What is the relative importance in the Jewish tradition, for example, of Chanukah and say, Pesach, the celebration of Passover, the Jewish liberation from Egypt? Why celebrate holidays at all? How should a society of many faiths and orientations present this array? What can people not committed to a specific faith gain from understanding the deep beliefs of others?

Another example of studying culture from close up and "in here" that is easily available to all is the study of language. This might take the form of surveying languages spoken in your school or neighborhood, or, if everyone speaks the "same" language, exploring slang, graffiti, and the dynamic nature of that language. One class made a list of terms and definitions that were less than ten years old. Another developed and administered to fellow students a "standardized test" for Black English:

Select the one correct usage:
  1. We straight.

     a. We are leaving.
     b. We are acting better.
     c. Everything is settled between you and me.
2. He been fix that car.
     a. He fixed that car a long time ago.
     b. He has been fixing that car.
     c. He is fixing that car.
3. They be hitting on peoples.
     a. They are hitting people.
     b. They hit on people all the time.
     c. They were hitting people.

June Jordan (1988) describes an astonishing process she observed while teaching a college course called "The Art of Black English," in which the class explored the uses, rules, and structures of a familiar but officially denigrated linguistic system. This class involved a lot of unlearning, a lot of moving beyond self-consciousness, a lot of creativity, and ultimately a dramatic encounter with life and death and the politics of language. During the semester, one of the students' brothers was killed by the police, and the class struggled with how to respond, how to adequately express their rage, grief, and identity. Whose language should be used? How could they be heard in their fullness? There was growth and change and surprise; the discovery of voice, and the enlargement of self.

Jordan points out that English is the "non-native currency of convenience" (p. 363) in over 33 countries, from Israel and Uganda to Zimbabwe and Malaysia. Further, in five countries with a total of 333,746,000 inhabitants, English is the native tongue. Her point is that "this thing called 'English'" is not the property of a specific class in a specific place, and that concepts of "standard English" are suspect, "strange and . . . tenuous" as she puts it. She notes that "the standard" held by the people in Malaysia, for example, is not the same as "the standard" in Zimbabwe, and concludes that "numerous forms of English now operate inside a natural, an uncontrollable, continuum of development" (p. 364).

A final example of studying culture from within a classroom might be an engagement with that most durable of cultural artifacts: the cultural stereotype. A stereotype, of course, is a kind of fixed metal plate for printing. A cultural stereotype is also fixed and unvarying—in this case it is an oversimplified belief that carries negative undercurrents. In our society, we can find visual and written reminders of all kinds of stereotypes: the lazy Mexican, the shiftless Negro, the inscrutable Chinese, the savage Indian, the greedy Jew. Our language is infused with them: "I was gypped," meaning I was cheated, as by Gypsies; "He is an Indian giver," meaning he is a cheat; "You're yellow," referring to Asian peoples, and meaning "cowardly." Most enduring are the terms associated with "black": black art (sorcery), black and blue (discolored from bruising), black ball (to exclude from membership), blackmail (to exhort by threats), black market (illicit trade), black out (enveloped in darkness), black heart (sinister or evil), black day (characterized by disaster), black mood (sad, gloomy, or calamitous), and so on.

There are all kinds of ways to study cultural stereotypes. One way is to discuss issues of fairness and inclusion and to enlist children in an anti bias campaign in the school or in the larger community. All children, even very young children, can become engaged in the pursuit of fairness and in trying to discover if books or other written materials are unfair or might hurt someone's feelings. Children can survey their own textbooks, collecting data in any number of forms: How many times are examples drawn from white, middle-class culture and how many times from other cultures? How many female as opposed to male characters in the books are engaged in meaningful work? How many African-Americans, whites, Latinos, or characters of other origins appear? And so on. The point is not to censor or create a test for any particular text; the point is to help children gain access to thinking actively and critically about their own learning and their own world.

A powerful entry into stereotypes is to begin with exactly the knowledge students bring to class. For example, after much discussion I often ask college students to think of and write down at least three cultural groups they belong to. Lists might include: Italian, Jewish, Mexican, Greek, African-American, Catholic, Baptist, female, gay, northsider, jocks, nerds, rappers, metal-heads, GQ's, blonds, geeks, and so on. I then ask them to write down a stereotype that other people generally have concerning those groups. In other words it is not an exercise in exposing stereotypes that pertain to you, or that you may have heard about others, but in describing what you know others sometimes say about you and your group. Making these issues public, discussing their history, the pain involved, and your awareness of them is a powerful lesson in cultural study. It has often provided luminous moments in my classroom.

Studying stereotypes in this way is not meant as an exercise by a teacher in delivering proclamations or conclusions to students. It is not meant as a way to replace an old orthodoxy with a new one. The teacher can be a guide, but she must also be willing to be a fellow inquirer. If she loses that stance, she will likely lose, as well, the ability to respond adequately to moments of real surprise and discovery for students. Further, in a study of this kind, trust and safety are essential—if students are uncovering evidence, it has one meaning; if they are being told how to think about these issues in particlar ways, it has a completely different meaning.

This context can provide opportunities for learning in depth. For example, when two sixth-graders got into an argument and knocked each other down, one called the other a "Polack," and he responded with "Nigger." Later one of the kids who had witnessed the fight asked which is worse, "Polack" or "Nigger." A discussion followed about the historical weight of words, about the relative power, say, of a German slurring both a Jew and an Italian, or of an Israeli slurring a German and a Palestinian. We talked, as well, about why African-Americans sometimes use "Nigger" among themselves as a term of endearment, how words can be co-opted and their meanings reversed, and how oppression can also be internalized. All the problems were not settled forever, but in this larger context of looking at cultural stereotypes, an unexpected incident became another opportunity for awareness and growth.

Bridge-building will be enhanced if the teacher structures time each week for a project of interest to students, something like the coming-of-age project discussed earlier in this chapter. This project might be initiated by the teacher, by the students, or through some interaction that incorporates the interests of both. It can come from a hobby, collection, an interest that students bring, a passion, or a question from the teacher. It can split the difference. It might be a whole-group undertaking, or a time for small groups, or for individual work. But in order to be effective, it must be structured into the life of the classroom—it must be part of the rhythm and routine, as in "Friday morning is project time."

Projects come from anywhere. One teacher I know in a Chicago public school was intrigued by a piece of junk mail she received: Subscribe to such-and-such magazine and get ten baby trees free. She discussed the proposition with her class, who became ignited by the prospect, and soon the tree project was in high gear. By the time the little trees arrived the class had figured out where to plant them, had researched tree biology, had discussed plans with the principal and with the parks department, and more. Soon there were tree collages and paintings, planting ceremonies, a poem by Joyce Carey, original poems, the film, "The Tree of the Wooden Clog," and more.

Remember José, the skateboarder, and the months spent trying to uncover an interest or a spark in this particularly challenging child? Seeing him outside of school, dazzling some neighborhood kids with his athleticism on a skateboard led to a subscription to Thrasher magazine, to a board design contest in class, and a skate-board repair shop with José as chief mechanic. Soon he was writing letters to the editor and researching the link between skateboards, roller skates, surfing, and skiing.

I no longer believe the old saying that you can learn something from anything. I now think, given the intense relationships and connections that exist everywhere, that you can learn everything from anything. The challenge is to take it deeper, to pursue it further, to search more carefully and more thoughtfully. Knowledge of the world presents itself whole. Teachers need to find ways to follow where it leads.

Lisa Delpit (1986, 1988) argues that an old debate in education, the debate between a "skill" and a "process" approach, is really a sterile and a false debate. Good teachers, she believes, incorporate all kinds of instructional strategies and are vigilant for "what works." Delpit thinks that underneath the "skills" versus "process" debate is discomfort and difficulty in recognizing or acknowledging "the culture of power."

The culture of power, she says, means that issues of power with specific rules for participation are enacted in classrooms, and that those issues reflect power relationships in the larger society. For example, the culture of power requires a certain amount of assertiveness and a certain amount of deference—knowing when to do what can be the kind of subtle knowledge teachers enact but fail to really understand or alert youngsters to. Similarly, the culture of power requires a certain type of language for certain situations—teaching kids explicitly when they must use "standard" English (and why) can be a germinal type of lesson for African-American children. In other words, "If you are not already a participant in the culture of power, being told explicitly the rules of that culture makes acquiring power easier" (Delpit, 1988, p. 282); and "those with power are frequently least aware of—or least willing to acknowledge—its existence. Those with less power are often most aware of its existence."

Delpit believes that children need to be taught the codes and rules for full participation, and that that teaching can only happen if teachers authentically seek out and consult parents and other adults who share the cultures of the children. She argues for communicating across cultures, a bridge-building activity that requires teachers to look, to listen, to open themselves to new ways of seeing and being: "We do not really see through our eyes or hear through our ears, but through our beliefs," Delpit says. "To put our beliefs on hold is to cease to exist as ourselves for a moment—and that is not easy. It is painful as well, because it means turning yourself inside out, giving up your sense of who you are, and being willing to see yourself in the unflattering light of another's angry gaze. It is not easy, but it is the only way to learn what it might feel like to be someone else and the only way to start the dialogue" (p. 297).

Delpit reminds us that each person is the expert on his or her own life; that the people with the problems are also likely to be the people with the solutions. She points us toward solidarity with the students we teach and their families, and away from smug superiority and patronization. She encourages us to study the history and reason within people's actions, to become explorers and ethnographers in the fullest sense. It becomes apparent, then, that multiculturalism is a political (as opposed to an anthropological) question; and that for teachers it is a question of democracy as well. The bridges we build can be stronger, more beautiful, more far-reaching than we had dared to imagine.

5

LIBERATING THE CURRICULUM

Curriculum is more than pieces of information, more than subject matter, more even than the disciplines. Curriculum is an ongoing engagement with the problem of determining what knowledge and experiences are the most worthwhile. With each person and with each situation, that problem takes on different shadings and meanings.

In the early days of my teaching I thought a lot about the curriculum. I examined what it was, and I wondered about what it could be and should be. I looked hard at the textbooks. They were limited in a thousand ways: uninteresting, irrelevant, written in a vapid, formulaic style, apparently by a committee of scholars intent on maximizing sales by offending no one. The result, of course, was a kind of muzak for the mind—easy listening some of the time, an annoying background buzz much of the time, catchy but not substantive. Underneath it all, the social studies and literature texts reflected and promoted white supremacy: There were no pictures or photographs of African Americans; there were no selections of Third World literature; there was throughout an assumed superiority and smug celebration of the status quo.

Everything in the curriculum—the books, materials, units, plans, and guides—was like this. It always felt a bit like fast food; it was available and a little addictive, filling, but in a disappointing kind of way, and you were hungry again soon after you finished. The curriculum had the same general relationship to knowledge or understanding as McDonald's has to nutrition. There is a link, weak and indirect and tentative though it may be.

My self-appointed task in those days was to find a better text—to pull out some fat and sugar, to pump some substance and fiber into those greasy burgers. And I was not entirely unsuccessful. For example, with my mentors BJ Richards and Denise Prince, I helped to develop a quick way for teachers to analyze racism in books, and to seek out alternatives. We built a library and then a bibliography of anti-bias books for children. And we collected a dazzling array of children's books that were good, solid literature. Our collection contained books by African-American, Native American, Latino, and Asian authors; books that mirrored for children, culturally and personally; books that stretched them and opened them to different or unfamiliar cultures and situations as well. We found books in which women as well as men were people of accomplishment, and where people of color as well as white people were able to solve problems, overcome obstacles, and think and act for the common good. And we found books that spoke of and to a wide range of experiences: a blind child describing her favorite spot on earth, a Native American child caring for goats on a farm, a child with a friend who has Down's Syndrome, an African child in a big, modern city, a child visiting a father in jail. We built an anti-bias library, a literature of diversity and inclusion.

This was only the beginning. All aspects of the curriculum were explored; everything was subjected to intense scrutiny. The point was to develop a curriculum that engaged kids, challenged them, encouraged them, activated them, and invited them to think seriously and deeply over a sustained period of time. We wanted a curriculum that opened all children to the possibility of a life lived with courage, hope, and love, or, as John Holt put it, to "a life worth doing" (Holt, 1990).

It took me awhile to discover that there were fundamental flaws in my journey—to realize that my baby steps forward kept occurring in the context of giant steps backward, and to figure out why it was so. This is not to say that my efforts in struggling for a better curriculum were completely wasted, or that the kind of exploration and scrutiny I participated in was entirely irrelevant. In fact, I think simply being engaged in that search made me a better, more aware teacher, and that my struggle with the curriculum brought life and purpose to my classroom. But the flaws demanded some attention.

There was, for example, the problem of the teacher's role in the curriculum. While my quest undoubtedly had a positive impact on my teaching, as soon as I began to think that I had figured it out, that my search was done, I would begin to slip back, to die as a teacher. In other words, the quest itself is really the thing worth doing—it is what infuses everything with energy and drive—not the completion, not the end-point. Furthermore, whatever insights I was gaining could not be transferred intact to inert teachers. If others became excited by the work, they reinvented and pursued it in their own ways and contexts; if not, it was just another of the millions of good ideas that wash over teachers all the time. There is no "teacher proof" curriculum that will humanize and energize the classroom of a deadly dull teacher—and there is no sense trying to find one.

Linked to this is the problem of the students' place in the curriculum. My own journey through the curriculum invited the students to come along as fellow travelers and co-conspirators. They became as interested in unearthing problems and developing alternatives as I had been. Critically examining the curriculum, in a sense, was our curriculum. It's an entirely different matter if a "better" curriculum is handed to passive students who are expected to swallow it whole. Once again, students meet it with indifference or hostility. Of course, the boring and irrelevant curriculum it is designed to replace was once considered by someone to be thoughtful, interesting, and hopeful. Inevitably, each one fails, not because of changing priorities or fads, but because of something more basically wrong.

What is basically wrong is this: The curriculum is considered to be "things," and these things amount to the stuff that some people have and other people need. Knowledge, thought, judgment, and wisdom are assumed to be the specific property of some expert, policy maker, or scholar who has predetermined and prepackaged it all for easy consumption. John Holt (1990) argues that the basic model of curriculum and teaching is "not just mistaken and impossible, but bad in the sense of morally wrong," because it is based on the idea "that some people have or ought to have the right to determine what a lot of other people know and think" (p. 275). This, he reminds us, is a profoundly undemocratic as well as a fatally flawed approach to pedagogy. Since knowledge is infinite, and knowing intersubjective and multidimensional, anyone who tries to bracket thinking in any definitive sense is, in essence, killing learning. Teachers can expose, offer, encourage, and stimulate—they should not dictate.

There are other, more hopeful ways to conceive the curriculum, and they all involve breaking barriers, unpacking preconceptions, exploding packages. Curriculum can be considered everything that goes on in a school, for example, not simply the material collected and delivered or the better package of goods, but all the unintended as well as planned consequences; all the hidden as well as overt messages; all the experienced as well as stated aspects of school life. Further, curriculum can be thought of as everything that goes on beyond as well as within the school walls. Schools, after all, are porous places, and the context of school is embedded in wider and wider circles of what some call the out-of-school curriculum (Schubert, 1986). Or, curriculum can be conceived in terms of an old and elegant question: What knowledge and experiences are of most value?

This fundamental curriculum question—what knowledge and experiences are most worthwhile—demands a dynamic response. That is, whatever answer one gives is necessarily tentative and contingent. It is understood as insufficient in some ways, uncertain in other ways, a single choice out of a thousand possible choices. Moreover, it will necessarily change each year, each month, each day possibly. As our son Malik learned to walk, his most worthwhile experience was walking. I remember following him for hours wandering around Central Park, this way and that, back and forth, falling down and getting up, concentrating on this one wonderful accomplishment. It would be a fairly inane "curriculum" for him now, but it is in fact the most worthwhile experience for my friend David, critically injured in a mountain climbing accident and now working, practicing, struggling as Malik once did, to simply walk.

Similarly, when he was on the cusp of reading, Malik needed good materials, opportunities, challenges, and encouragement as he crossed into the world of competent and enthusiastic readers. In those days, we did a lot of reading together, some common sense phonics, a bit of word identification, lots of writing. Malik now reads the way a fish swims in water—he is surrounded by it, he breathes it, he is largely unaware of it, except as a medium to propel him where he is heading. It would be hopeless and rather stupid to build a curriculum around phonics or word identification for Malik today. But that is a reasonable and responsible thing to do with Malik's friend Bob, who has struggled with reading for a range of reasons and is now eager and ready to catch up.

And so it goes. Think of your own childhood learning, or think of yourself today. Think of the overlapping circles of knowledge, experience, and need. There are always things that demand to be learned in life, always next challenges and goals. If you can separate the learning from the credentialling process of schooling, you will remember moments when the most important thing was to understand some phenomenon or to master some skill. The curriculum of sixth grade may have been to prepare us for seventh grade, but for many of us, our energy was drawn urgently to other worthwhile knowledge and experiences: learning to dance, perhaps, or building model airplanes, or pursuing a favorite author, or mastering fashion, or earning money.

Even now, there are things that demand to be known: I learned to repair bicycles because it was a necessary step in my devotion to riding; my friend Murray became an expert on Alzheimer's disease because his wife suffers from it; too many people have learned more than they wanted to know about biology, immunology, and oncology because of the rampaging epidemic of AIDS.

Almost everyone I know has figured out how to use a personal computer because it emerged as valuable to them in their lives. And most people I know have idiosyncratic needs and desires on their curriculum/learning agendas this year: Chris and Leslie are studying Spanish, Ann is reading about allergies and alternative medicines, Eli is building an environment for turtles, Brenda is learning to write for a wider audience, Jeanette is cramming for her citizenship test, Kaki is collecting original editions of books by Holling Clancy Holling. The most worthwhile knowledge and experience in an infinitely expanding universe turn out to be various.

This makes life in classrooms incredibly complicated and yet endlessly fascinating. Elementary school teachers need to visit and revisit the basic curriculum question regularly, and, as before, their best allies in this pursuit are the students themselves. What knowledge and experiences are most worthwhile? Finding ways to ask that question of students in a number of different contexts is the surest way to keep the curriculum on track, and has the added advantage of provoking students from passivity to creative engagement, from indifference to responsible activity, from aimlessness to reflection and wonder at the scope and diversity of a life worth living. In one class, I might interview each child over a period of days: What do you want to learn in kindergarten? In another, I might print the basic curriculum question in bold letters on cardboard and post it on the wall for ready reference. In any case, if the question is understood and embraced, the teacher has created a useful framework for students to think about their own thinking, to engage in conscious choice-making on their intellectual journies, their pathways to greater knowledge, skills, and ability.

This does not mean that anything goes, or that the teacher disappears. On the contrary, the teacher has a bigger responsibility to create a dynamic and flexible classroom, and to build challenge and exposure into each school day. Still, youngsters need opportunities to choose, to name, and to pursue their own passions and projects, to develop some part of the class as their own. It is in the interaction of teacher and student, of immediate interest and larger purpose, that a living curriculum can be forged.

On the other hand, if the question of worthwhile knowledge and experience is side-stepped or ignored, it emerges through another door. That is, saying that the question is "none of my business," "not my job," or "just philosophy," allows the question to be answered outside of the people most directly impacted by it. Every school, classroom, routine, and schedule, every unit and lesson plan embodies an answer to the question of what is worthwhile. Perhaps this helps to explain why so many youngsters conclude that school itself is useless. School is the place where they act as if the most worthwhile experience is sitting quietly or practicing repetitive tasks until your mind aches; where the most worthwhile knowledge is presented as disconnected fragments of information.

Teachers have another challenge, and one that is connected to remaining aware of the question of what is most worthwhile. They must also link that question with a fundamental teaching question: How do I create the conditions for children to have full access to those valuable experiences and that worthwhile knowledge? What activities, materials and resources can give children opportunities to choose that knowledge and those experiences? The answer to this question is equally dynamic and complex. There is no formula or recipe that works for all learners in all times. There is no set of lesson plans or units that can engage the range of learning styles, approaches, and intelligences that are likely to gather in any given classroom. Once again, the teacher is thrust back on herself; she must find ways to draw on the full range of her own resources, her intelligence, skill, and experiences, as she invents her teaching anew. And she can, if she is secure enough and wise enough, unleash the latent power before her, drawing forth the resources of the students themselves.

When I realized that no curriculum unit was ever good enough (even though many materials and resources are terrific and worth drawing on) and that I needed to focus on curriculum as a living challenge rather than as a better package, I began to evolve a framework for deliberating about curriculum in my own classrooms. I wanted to be proactive in thinking about curriculum, not always reacting to guidelines or requirements or units coming at me from the outside. Furthermore, I wanted to measure my teaching against something more substantive than whether my class was "well-managed," and whether the scope and sequence expectations were fulfilled. I'd seen too many teachers sacrifice their larger purposes and either quit teaching altogether or turn themselves into the teacher they swore they'd never be. I needed something more than this to pin my teaching on.

I'm not certain where or when I got each piece of my framework for thinking about the curriculum. And I'm not sure it will always look as it does today. But I do know struggling with the following questions helps me as I move along in my teaching:

- *Are there opportunities for discovery and surprise?* I'm interested in students constructing their own knowledge and feeling powerful and energized enough to go further in their expectations of the world and their own minds. We all worry about motivation and self-esteem—I can testify that the motivation and self-esteem that come from discovery and real accomplishment make the motivational posters of Michael Jordan that read, "Stay in School," look silly. I want to be sure that my curriculum, whatever else it does, provides opportunities to make discoveries.
- *Are students actively engaged with primary sources and hands-on materials?* I want children to explore the world in order to take meaning from it and to make sense of it. I'm not interested in their feeding on predigested materials; I want them to get right up next to what they're studying, to touch it and smell it. Slavery as a few pages in a textbook is sanitized and smooth, but slave narratives, actual bills of sale, and Congressional debates—that's more like it.
- *Is productive work going on?* Much of the "work" of school is not work at all—it is make-work or busy-work, meaningless stuff to occupy our time. Everyone is eager for the day to end, for the term to end, for the year to end. This is preparation for meaningless jobs, I guess, which we also wait out, wishing they would end, as we experience time ticking away and our lives coming to an end, in isolated desperation. In contrast, I'm interested in work that is purposeful and engaging, for me and for my students. I'm interested in the dignity of work, and in the human desire to prove your existence through your work. I want some of our classwork to be work that is good for the school—a school store or printshop or garden—and some that is helpful to our neighborhood—a class ecology project or volunteer community service project. I also want to make the work of teaching visible to my students so that they know it is not

idiotic, and I want them to see me involved in the pursuit of my own questions, and to see me as a collaborator in pursuit of their questions as well.

- *Is the work linked to student questions or interests?* I'm concerned that school be a welcoming place, a creative place for students to work on their own concerns. A lot of what goes on in school is of the "take-this-pill-because-I-know-it's-good-for-you" variety. I don't want my class to drive children out; rather I want to develop my agenda in light of theirs.

- *Are problems within the classroom, the school, and the larger community part of student consciousness?* I don't know all the answers. Not only do I not know how to solve big problems like war or environmental degradation, I don't even know how to solve problems like how to explain long-division in a way that really helps Jamie, or how to get Pat to stop hitting people when he's angry. What I can do is allow problems to surface, frame issues for discussion, create conditions for Jamie's friends to assist her, and bring my own concerns to the group about Pat. Through peer teaching, small groups, circle or meeting time, we can take on real problems together and strive for real solutions. Our classroom can be, among other things, a children's workshop on divergent thinking. Nothing is simple.

- *Is work in my classroom pursued to its far limits?* I often wonder if we couldn't go one more step, ask one more question, bring in one more resource person, take one more trip, figure out one more activity. I worry that too much of what kids experience in school is skimming along the surface of knowledge and never really plunging in. Some teachers say, "Make it simple," but my job is keeping it complex. And to do that, I need to see that in many instances, "less is more," that is, covering a zillion items may not be as rewarding as pursuing something fully, deeply, truly, and well.

There must be more. I still need to look back at my larger purposes and goals. I still need to figure out how to assess how we are doing along the way. But for me these are the basics, and this is a beginning. Posting these questions on the wall makes me more thoughtful, more focused.

————————

Let me take this one step further. If teachers embrace these new basics as benchmarks for their own teaching, they simultaneously free themselves from a host of difficulties, and open themselves to a range of different challenges. New challenges include how to respond to mandated guidelines, how to know what is working without reference to tidy if meaningless indicators, how to demonstrate to colleagues and the wider school community that your teaching is legitimate and worthwhile, how to keep track of student progress. One old concern, however, may fall away: Integrating the curriculum will not be a tough issue because the curriculum has not been segregated. More important, my attention can be liberated from a focus on discreet skills, test scores, and classroom management; I can now look at issues of more immediate and authentic relevance to learning. That's a relief.

Entry points are everywhere. Alice Jefferson, a veteran teacher I know, decides each summer to do a sustained study with her class the next year on a subject she knows nothing about. "That's not much of a challenge," Alice laughs, "since I know nothing about so many things." She insists that this special study keeps her alive as a teacher—intellectually engaged, curious, interested, learning all the time.

One year, Alice picked "whales," another year it was "quilting," and another it was "paper." She announces early in the school year that there will be, along with everything else, a special study of her designated topic. She arranges one table as an "interest table" around the study—a place where students can bring their discoveries—one bookshelf for books and materials related to it, and sets aside some time to work on projects relevant to the special topic. "The astonishing thing," she reports, "is that the year I chose 'penguins' there were penguins on the cover of both the *National Geographic* and *Ranger Rick*, and the year I chose 'steel,' the *New Yorker* and *Smithsonian* did special features on the manufacture of steel. Whatever I choose, the children get charged up and we seem to find it everywhere."

This is not really so astonishing. The special topics Alice chooses to keep herself alive as a teacher are large and available. They are in the world and therefore they are of interest to more people than just her. Furthermore, they energize her students in part because her own energy is so obvious and so engaging. She has taken herself out of the I-know-you-don't stance, and created an ethos of collective inquiry; this new stance allows students to enact learning in powerful, new ways.

Another teacher I know, Joan Cenedella, spends part of each summer designing a "core study"—the core is a way to investigate the human world through reading, mapping, writing, the arts, science, math, and history. Through the core, interrelated concepts—survival, community, continuity, search for meaning, values, change—can be examined and reexamined in ever-widening contexts. One year, the core was "Exploring Environments," another year it was "Native People," and another it was "Justice." Joan invested a lot of effort in each core study she developed, searching for primary sources, developing ideas for activities, linking together imaginative literature with anthropological or scientific materials, and webbing it all together into an intricate and complex design.

No matter how much preliminary work she did, however, the core always grew and changed once the children got their hands on it. The most dramatic reversal occurred one year when the core study was to be "Immigration." Joan's plan included spending a couple of days exploring a New York City street corner, which in her mind embodied the intersection of cultures and peoples. This would lead, she thought, to some mapping, some interviewing, writing, research, and more. Soon they would be reading about Henry Hudson, slavery, waves of European immigration, Puerto Rico, and on and on.

The children enjoyed the street corner, but one child kept looking westward and asking, "Can we go see the river?" Other children glanced west, too, and soon there was a groundswell of interest in visiting the river. And so, when they finished drawing in their trip books, handy little spiral notebooks that accompanied them everywhere, they went to the river's edge for a snack. While they were there, someone said, "Look, the river is flowing up," and another responded, "No, it has to flow south—down." When the children turned to Joan for an answer, she wasn't sure, and so they talked about how they might find out.

These were the opening shots of a core study of the river. This study took several months, and involved experiments with water flow and "Pooh sticks," trips to a nature preserve on the river north of the city, reconstructions of natural features found along the river, interviews with naturalists, a class-sponsored, school-wide treasure hunt at the river's edge, and much more. When the class turned their attention back to Henry Hudson, they had discovered for themselves that the Hudson River is a tidal river, that it flows both north and south, and they had visited the exact spot where the tide stops its northward push. That was exciting.

At La Escuela Fratney, a public school in Milwaukee, Wisconsin, the entire school community, including students, develops central themes that will guide the work of every grade and class for the school year. For 1990–1991, the themes were:

We Respect Ourselves and Our World
   a. Every living thing has needs.

    b. I am somebody important.
    c. We all have a cultural heritage.
    d. We need to live in peace.
We Send Messages When We Communicate
    a. Communication is two-way.
    b. We communicate in many languages and in many ways.
    c. Stereotypes are contained in cartoons, books, magazines and TV.
    d. TV can be dangerous to our health.
We Can Make a Difference on Planet Earth
    a. We have been shaped by the past, we shape the future.
    b. African-American people have contributed greatly to our nation.
    c. We celebrate the contributions of women.
    d. People of all nationalities have worked for justice and equality.
    e. We need to overcome prejudice and racism.
We Share Stories of the World
    a. My family's story is important.
    b. We learn about other people through their stories.
    c. We can all be storytellers and actors.

                                       (La Escuela Fratney, 1991, p. 41)

The themes at Fratney are big enough to allow for endless variation and initiative in each class and by every teacher and student, and yet focused enough to create a lot of interaction and cross-group learning—and a very yeasty mix. "We need to live in peace" involved creating some guidelines for conflict-resolution in one first grade class, and an inquiry into military budgets in one sixth-grade class. "We learn about other people through their stories" meant reading fairy tales from around the world in a kindergarten class, and interviewing Native Americans throughout Wisconsin in a fifth-grade class. This is the strength and the beauty of picking a theme, or several themes, around which to organize a school or a classroom. The theme stretches and challenges everyone, even as it directs and focuses energy.

In my classroom, themes would often emerge from the children, and I would be running to catch up, making connections, asking challenging questions, arranging next steps. One such theme resulted from a spontaneous discussion of our families and the realization that Stephanie was the middle of seven children while James was an only child; that Marcus had a black father and white mother while Joy had a black mother and a white father; that Tony's father was in jail and that Sean had two mothers. The theme was "All Kinds of Families."

Sometimes themes grew from community events. A conflict in our neighborhood between old residents and a wave of new arrivals led to the theme, "Everyone Has Neighbors." The closing of a neighborhood hospital and the resulting upheaval resulted in the theme, "Speaking of Health and Medicine."

Sometimes I initiated a theme. For example, living in New York City, I had been interested in a particular loss of perspective that comes from an intensely urban experience. It was fascinating to me that New Yorkers routinely dismissed the fact that there was a serious and real drought occurring, that their source of water was dangerously low, and that no one was able to slow people's wasting of water. After all, when you turned on the faucet, water poured out, so everything must be fine, and who, after all, believed the mayor or the governor? It was kind of like people centuries ago watching the sun rise and set, and knowing we lived on a flat surface with this fire-ball circling overhead. One day, Sarah's mother and I were talking after school, and the eruption of Mount St. Helen's in Washington came up. She said, "I can't believe this is happening in twentieth-century America." Volcanoes, earthquakes, nature itself had become for her something that belonged to a less technological age, or to an underdeveloped country. I began to work on a theme for the following year on nature and survival—a theme I came to call "Living on the Land/Living in the City."

Pursuing themes like these requires a lot of work—much more work for a teacher than delivering lessons—and vastly expanded work from students. The year we worked on "Living on the Land/Living in the City," we created a garden in a vacant lot, raised rabbits in the room, plotted fault lines and studied something of plate tectonics, developed a school-wide recycling plan, compared the Sioux approach to hunting with Buffalo Bill's, traveled to the huge port of entry for farm products into the city, led a campaign to board up an abandoned building, interviewed community residents for our newsletter about survival, mapped the cultures in our neighborhood, and built a spaceship for intergalactic travel. The spaceship was a lot of fun and it underlined an important issue we were struggling with—we are all dependent on the land, on food, air, and water—no matter where we live—and while the city can mask that fact, nowhere is our dependence more obvious than when we leave the earth altogether. We must then find ways to literally take her with us. Space travel, like city living, doesn't solve the problem of wasting our natural resources; it holds our problems up for us in sharp relief.

This theme, of course, provided multiple opportunities for discovery and surprise—plotting fault lines was the first occasion I ever had for really understanding how scientists figured out plate movement. Some children discovered a lot about animals, others were surprised by the cultural diversity in our neighborhood. There were opportunities for active learning, for going out and investigating, interviewing, touching the things under consideration. A lot of what we did was real work—work with a purpose. For example, we raised lettuce and tomatoes in our garden, and we petitioned the city to close a dangerous building. This kind of work enhanced everything else we did— even some of the tedious and necessary classroom tasks. And we returned again and again to the interests of the students—we built the spaceship because several boys wanted to do that; we developed our recycling plan at Ariel and Megan's suggestion.

When some part of school life is organized this way, the collateral benefits can be breathtaking. Youngsters have a sense that knowledge is vast and open-ended—there is always more to wonder about, more to feast on, more to explore. School stops being the place of simple-minded conclusions and thin gruel. And time stops being something to pass, and becomes more hopeful, more precious.

Furthermore, students begin to learn in the way the young have learned from the beginning of time—by following along in the footsteps of someone older and more competent. Lillian Weber, founder of the Workshop Center at City College in New York and an extraordinarily powerful teacher, points out that following along is the traditional way of learning in a family—following the work of kitchen or shop, child rearing or mending, story telling, myth making or Bible reading. As the work of families becomes scattered or dissipated or rationalized and invisible, children lose a valuable resource in their growth and development. Allowing some of the work of school to be visible and available means that youngsters can find a place to follow along once again.

Finally, children are the great untapped resource in most schools. Instead of unlocking the energy of hundreds of people gathered together each day, most schools spend additional resources containing and controlling kids. A school that engages youngsters in creating a better school and a better community taps a vast reservoir of talent, energy, and labor. Liberating the energy of youngsters is hard work, and I don't mean to romanticize it or pretend it can be simply decreed—many teachers have retreated to more traditional approaches when they found it was much, much harder than they'd ever imagined. But it can be done. Projects like those described above involved children in serious school and community service. Since nothing appeals more to a child than to be of use, projects can become important channels for concentrated activity and vibrant connections to other work. Projects become, as well, powerful vehicles for learning social responsibilities and practicing life in a democratic community.

With all this in mind, it is worth attending to another important matter in schools—the old, basic skills. Perhaps we have developed by now a broader perspective on learning, and we can avoid the sterile educational debate about skills versus process. Perhaps we can make our own way into the critical matter of reading, writing, and arithmetic without prejudice or alarm. Perhaps we can acknowledge the value of skills without erasing what we know about the worth of persons or the importance of connectedness in teaching. Perhaps.

Of course, if some part of classroom life is structured around a theme, a core study, a special topic, then, as we saw, basic skills are necessarily already engaged. Not only are skills like reading, writing, and arithmetic needed to pursue these projects, but they emerge and are taught in context. Reading is not, then, a skill without a goal; reading is the connection of the world and the word, a powerful and essential tool. Geography and history are no longer merely maps, names, and dates, but become ways of locating oneself in time and space, uncovering silences and recreating connections, developing a narrative of change. Math and science, far from lists and facts and drills, are vital entry points into pattern, order, continuity and discontinuity within and beneath our experience. In every case the point is to ignite the imagination, an essential force for thinking about any of this, to restore life to thought, and to build the wide range of literacies needed for full engagement with and participation in the modern world.

When the talk turns to skills, too many educators become simple-minded. A clear and readily available example is the system-wide learning objectives, curriculum guidelines, or state mandates. Consistently written in a tight, instrumentalist language, they precipitate intellectual claustrophobia. Here, for example, is how Illinois describes its goals and purposes in teaching the social sciences:

> As a result of their schooling, students will be able to:
> - understand and analyze comparative political and economic systems, with an emphasis on the political and economic systems of the United States;
> - understand and analyze events, trends, personalities, and movements shaping the history of the world, the United States and Illinois;
> - demonstrate a knowledge of the basic concepts of the social sciences and how these help to interpret human behavior;
> - demonstrate a knowledge of world geography with emphasis on that of the United States;
> - apply the skills and knowledge gained in the social sciences to decision making in life situations.
>
> (Illinois State Board of Education, 1986, p. v)

As a teacher, the certainty of this writing always annoys me. "As a result of their schooling, students will be able to. . . . " I always want to add "maybe, with a lot of luck," or ask them how they can be so sure. And when it turns out that as a result of their schooling, students don't understand and analyze events, what then? The assumption seems to be that if we say it neat and clean, the job is done. If the kids don't get it, it's their fault; give them bad grades and move on.

Lesson plans use the identical formulation for every sub-skill and tiny behavior. It all claims too much for schooling, of course, as if school is all there is to a child's experience. It turns out that Thai, at age six, demonstrated a vast knowledge of world geography—he thinks like a cartographer and his dad is an amateur explorer—while Timmy, at ten, isn't much of a map reader—he's busy with other things. As a result of their schooling, both are bored stiff, but one reads maps, the other builds rockets.

The next step is even nuttier. Here the state offers twenty-four model learning objectives (for the fifth outcome statement, listed above) for the end of the third grade. For example:

- Give examples of choices of activities to fill a need.
- Choose between two products to help reach an important goal.
- Recognize that every course of action has consequences.
- Know actions have consequences.
- Give examples of persons as consumers, persons as producers, and persons as citizens.
- Recognize the factors influencing a person's relationship with others, e.g., age, emotion, and genetics.
- Distinguish between positive and negative relationships.
- Recognize that the worker provides goods and services.
- Recognize that all forms of work require training.

(pp. 55–57)

These kinds of goals and objectives present teachers with a serious, though not impossible challenge. The challenge is to teach well in spite of the mandates, to refuse the implied constraints and confinements and to do a good job with students anyway. The most straightforward way I know to accomplish this is to begin somewhere else. That is, whenever you get a mandate or guideline, set it aside until you have sketched out your large purposes and goals, and filled those in with specific plans and concrete action steps. At this point, you can refer to the guidelines without cringing before them.

After I had generated a lot of ideas and done a lot of reading, thinking, and planning around my project, "Living on the Land/

Living in the City," I picked up the official curriculum guidelines and checked off the objectives I covered. On this occasion, and virtually each time I've done this, I discovered something interesting: The official guidelines (which can seem so huge in the abstract) are literally overwhelmed by my larger purposes, and surpassed in every particular. For example, here are sample learning objectives from the Illinois guidelines for language arts:

> As a result of their schooling, students will be able to write standard English in a grammatical, well-organized and coherent manner for a variety of purposes.

> By the end of GRADE 6, students should be able to:
> A1. Know the purposes of public and personal writing.
> A2. Use the various forms of public and personal writing.
> A3. Write for various audiences.
> B1. Focus clearly upon one central idea or event when writing.
> B2. Use information from other sources when writing.
> C1. Use descriptive details, reasons for an opinion, concrete examples of solutions to problems when writing.
> D1. Write in narrative, expository, descriptive and persuasive styles.
> D2. Use transitional words for time-order and comparison/ contrast when writing.
> E1. Write using conventional forms of standard English.
> E2. Use the dictionary when unsure about the spelling of a word.
> F1. Review a piece of writing to correct spelling, punctuation and grammar.
> F2. Do simple revisions to meet the needs of audience and purpose.
> (p. 30)

In our project, kids wrote a lot: journals, letters to neighbors, interview protocols, petitions, surveys, complaints, a newsletter, and more. Yes, they experienced public and personal writing, and yes, they struggled with conventional forms of standard English. They did more than this: They debated the subtle meanings of words, a few wrote a play, some invented names for parts of the spaceship. Amazingly, they were not yet in the sixth grade.

Students also recognized the dependence of living things on the earth (an Illinois science objective). Building the spaceship and trying to figure out what to bring was incredibly enlightening. And, of course, pleasant and unpleasant environmental conditions (another Illinois objective) are a part of all of our lives, and became an ongoing matter for reflection among my students.

The point is that any single objective can be simply an obvious part of something larger and fuller, or it can be sought out and brought onto center stage and taught didactically as if it held some magic power in and of itself. A week spent on using the dictionary or on public and personal writing would about finish me off; a lecture on environments would be an object lesson in unpleasantness. On the other hand, the interviews, surveys, and work at hand sent us regularly to the dictionary, a skill that became vital to our own purposes—check that objective off as covered.

Another way to meet the problem of guidelines and mandates is to give them to the students. Again, after some work and effort, some development of environment, community, and goals, a teacher can simply call a meeting and explain to the kids what the district (the city, the state, the federal government) expects to happen in this class. She can hand out copies of the guidelines to the students, discuss everything—the language, the implications, the underlying assumptions—and ask the kids to help figure out where to go. Their intelligence, creativity, and irreverent inventiveness can be brought to bear in solving a real challenge, and the result can be terrific. An added advantage is that this allows students access to the larger framework in which their schooling occurs.

With few exceptions, all children can learn to read. Some seem to learn easily and effortlessly; others struggle with reading. Some learn quickly and early in life, while some take a long time. Zayd could read "pizza" on the signs above restaurants when he was three, and he read simple story books at five. Malik didn't read until he was seven, and then all at once. Chesa approached reading in a workman-like manner, struggling with whole words and phonics simultaneously. Like child birth, no two are exactly the same. Many children begin to read at four or five, and many do not read until seven or eight—neither alone indicates anything about intelligence, ability, or potential. There is no particular virtue in reading early and effortlessly, no particular problem in learning to read later and as a result of hard work.

In any case, children do learn to read, and reading is quite a dazzling accomplishment—readers have figured out that printed symbols carry messages, that when groups of letters are stable they mean the same thing always, and that words can be analyzed and unraveled to discover meaning. Reading is a sophisticated and complex cognitive

process, and children experience real pleasure when they put it all together and read.

Unfortunately, the focus on reading problems and difficulties, and
the academic debates swirling around reading, have overshadowed
much of what makes sense about reading, and have mystified learning
to read. Over the past decades, researchers have made important contributions in our understanding of the problems faced by the tiny
number of youngsters who are neurologically impaired—but in many
instances these contributions have been erased by anxious parents and
teachers who uncover "soft neurological signs" everywhere they look.
Psychologists have understood a lot about the reading difficulties of
the small number of emotionally disturbed youngsters—but again,
these insights are undermined by adults seeking professional intervention for every five-year-old not reading. "Dyslexia"—a word that has
entered the mainstream of school-talk and is thrown around like con-
fetti—simply means "reading difficulty." But when someone says,
"Joe is dyslexic," it sounds like an objective scientific determination
or a death sentence. Likely, the truth is that Joe is learning to read
more slowly, and the hyper-expectation and over-emphasis on remedi-
ation won't help him or anyone else.

The age-old phonics versus non-phonics debate has added a lot
of heat, if little light, to the problem. Proponents of a phonics approach to teaching children to read are eager for youngsters to break
the code, to get the skill, and to become independent readers; they
argue for moving from the specific to the general, from letter sounds
to blends to words to sentences, and they assume that a sense of
meaning and the power of reading will come in time. Those in favor
of a "whole-word," "language experience," or "whole-language" approach move from the general to the specific, and they reason that
once the power of language, reading, and writing are understood, the
relationship of letters and sounds will also emerge. While the debate
is often fierce, usually backed up with lots of anecdotal evidence and
studies cited, the truth is that effective teachers succeed with either
approach, or with some other approach altogether. This is because
reading is picked up here and there from a range of experiences and
activities; the specific approach or technique of a given teacher is not
isolated from the world or even from other things occurring in the
classroom.

This is not to say that the debate is meaningless. On the contrary,
just as an obsession with neatness in writing can kill the desire to
express oneself on paper, an undue stress on letter-sound combina-
tions can strip away the power of meaning. Most reading experts ar-

gue that there is not one best approach for all children at all times, and that effective teachers need every technique at their fingertips in order to invent the best approach for each particular child. The debate, though, reminds me of an observation made by Sue Hubbell (1988) in her lovely account of her journey as a beekeeper:

> Beekeepers are an opinionated lot, each sure that his methods, and his methods alone, are the proper ones. When I first began keeping bees, the diversity of passionately held opinion bewildered me, but now that I have hives in locations scattered over a thousand-square-mile area I think I understand it. . . . Frosts come earlier in some places than in others. Spring comes later. Rainfall is not the same. The soils, and the flowering plants they support, are unlike. Through the years, I have learned that as a result of all these variations I must keep the bees variously. Most people who keep bees have only a few hives, and have them all in one place. They find it difficult to understand why practices that have proved successful for them do not work for others. But I have learned that I must treat the bees in one yard quite differently from the way I do those even thirty miles away. The thing to do, I have discovered, is to learn from the bees themselves. (p. 45)

Learning from the bees themselves means that teachers have certain general responsibilities: They must create a literate environment (this is especially important where the home or school community is not filled with books, newspapers, magazines, and people reading); they must structure a lot of time and space for reading, writing, and speaking; they must embody literacy in their own activities by reading aloud, telling stories, and reading quietly in class every day. If children have a literate environment, opportunities to read, something to read for, an audience for their reading and writing and speaking, and a teacher who knows how to pull teaching techniques from a wide repertoire of possibilities—all children can learn to read.

Math and science present a different set of problems for teachers. While proponents of a hands-on and integrated approaches to math and science make a vigorous argument for change, there is no real opposition except inertia and fear. Many teachers resort to a "drill and kill" approach out of a sense of incompetence in math and science. Math phobia is a common affliction of teachers, and something that must be resisted if strong and able students is our goal.

One way to resist is to approach math as a functional and concrete expression of the world, not as a verbal or highly abstract set of operations. Math is about pattern and relationship, as is science. Since we already know that math expresses patterns and relationships in abstract terms, we often leap too quickly to a level where students become lost and we ourselves struggle.

Our own confusion about math can be an important aid in our teaching, if we take it seriously. Instead of staying on the abstract plane, passing out work-sheets we ourselves only vaguely understand, insisting on endless repetition, we can challenge ourselves to return to the beginning, to play with pattern and relationship using geoboards, cuisenaire rods, unifix cubes, unit blocks, rubber bands. We can manipulate numbers and things, count, order, reorganize, construct, and contrast. We can stop pursuing examples and reiterations, and begin to try to measure the world or tell our stories in math. We can keep a math journal. In short, we can build up our own math knowledge from the concrete to the abstract, from the first-hand to the more distant, from the cumulative to the analytical—and in this way, we can perhaps better understand a student's journey into mathematical thinking. If we understand the direction of that learning, we can account for it in our teaching of others—we are less likely to repeat the rules for long division more loudly, and more likely to pull out a geoboard.

Children are naturally curious about the world we inhabit. They want to explore the biosphere, the woods, the railroad tressle, the park. They are interested in more and less, far and near, big and small, before and after lunch, long before they know that "fiveness" is an abstraction that can stand by itself. Then they are interested in what to do with this standing-alone five. Teachers can tap into this interest easily: How many fives can you make out of this batch of crayons? How strong is string? Do the cracks in the sidewalk form a pattern? Where do the pigeons live? Why does gum stick to the bottom of chairs? If I pop this popcorn with no top on the pan, will it fall in a pattern? On and on.

Nothing in the curriculum is entirely neutral, not even sports, not even the weather. These are often the favored examples pulled from a world of possibilities when youngsters begin to learn about statistics. Who could object? But choosing the weather as a vehicle for statistical analysis means excluding something else—a statistical study of unemployment by race, for example; a statistical look at state spending on education by community; a statistical portrait of access to adequate health care by income. Pursuing the study of statistics in light of larger problems and social issues provides opportunities to extend and expand the curriculum, but also to grab the interests and commitments of youngsters struggling to understand the world and their place in it.

Just as becoming literate with words requires a certain environment, stance, and approach, so becoming literate in math and science makes similar demands: an environment rich in math and science possibilities (graphs, charts, time-lines, schedules, puzzles, maps, scales, animals, plants, manipulative materials, measuring tools), opportunity to work with number and pattern and relationship, and an expectation that math and science can be an engaging and powerfully generative way to know the world. We can again develop particular projects: After months of playing a variety of board games in the third grade, each child might spend several weeks creating his or her own board game, and then teach it to the third graders down the hall; after much interest in environmental waste, the sixth grade might hold a school-wide contest to design a package that will not end up in a landfill and yet will keep two raw eggs from breaking when dropped from the roof. As before, one child will learn about pulleys from constructing them, another from reading about them in books. The point is not for the teacher to choose, but to allow both possibilities, and even more.

Social studies offers another kind of problem for teachers. The subject does not engender a great debate, as in reading, nor a fear and loathing, as with math and science. In social studies, the problem is that the content is undefined and watery, that it covers everything and nothing. For this reason, teachers use social studies as a curriculum catch-all, and the meaning of the social studies typically eludes students.

Social studies draws on all the social sciences—sociology and psychology, anthropology and economics, political science, geography, and history—but it coheres around a single question: How do human beings interact with one another and their environment? This is a question children of all ages are grappling with directly and immediately. Entry points into the social studies are everywhere: families, neighborhoods, current events, gangs, work, food.

Mapping spaces can be a useful starting point and can become increasingly sophisticated over time. Youngsters can collect various maps of their city or community as a way to understand the multiple purposes of mapping. The typical street map is only a beginning. In my kindergarten class in New York City, we had maps from the sanitation department showing pick-up routes and dumps; from the power company indicating sub-stations and average usage; from the chamber of commerce illustrating consumer patterns; from the public transportation department describing bus and train lines. We collected maps of parks, maps of houses of worship, maps of community income, maps of neighborhood festivals, ethnic and racial maps.

Since mapping is a visual description of some dimension of human or physical relationships, youngsters can be challenged to make maps of their own concerns: map the earth according to destruction of the natural environment; map the national expenditure on weaponry or social programs; map the world according to food production and projected population.

One innovative teacher organized a group of sixth-graders to be "young ethnographers" and to take down the life histories or autobiographical narratives of kindergartners. These accounts became reading books, histories, cultural studies, and more. These kids later moved on to "elder interviews" in the neighborhood, and challenged themselves not only to tell a story, but to tell why a person's story is important, and to use a variety of sources to get it told. Another teacher led her third-graders in a survey of community attitudes about public transportation. A third had his fifth-graders trading an imaginary thousand dollars start-up money on the New York stock exchange. This project took an interesting and unexpected turn the year one boy refused to trade Coca-Cola because of its involvement with South Africa. Soon the study included apartheid and foreign economic policy, sweat shops and the role of labor, child labor in the history of the United States, and more.

Once again, an environment that encourages geographic and historical thinking; a courageous and caring teacher; an opportunity to pursue questions in breadth and depth—these are the elements that allow students access to literacy in the social studies.

———————

Stokely Carmichael taught classes in a Freedom School organized by the Student Nonviolent Coordinating Committee (SNCC) in Mississippi in the early 1960s.[1] Freedom Schools grew out of the civil rights struggle as a vehicle for community education and involvement, and Stokely was famous as a Freedom School teacher in Mississippi long before he was nationally known as the leader who embodied the shift toward Black Power and greater militancy within the movement. Stokely's classes always began with some acknowledgment of what the students themselves knew, then traveled over new, often surprising terrain as students discovered, constructed, and connected with things not yet known. It was exciting to be in Stokely's classes; challenging, funny, sometimes troubling, always lively. One class began with Stokely writing several sentences opposite one another on the chalkboard:

I digs wine	I enjoy drinking cocktails
The peoples want freedom	The people want freedom
I wants to reddish to vote	I want to register to vote
	(Stembridge, 1971, pp. 3–4)

Students laughed and teased as they watched him write. Stokely asked them what they thought of the two sets of sentences. One student said "peoples" didn't sound right. Stokely asked if they knew what "peoples" meant, if they knew anyone who said "peoples." Several students replied that everyone knew what it meant and that they knew many people, including themselves, who said "peoples" and often spoke sentences like those in the left column. But, added one, it isn't "correct English." Stokely then asked them who decides questions of correct and incorrect, and this exchange followed:

STOKELY: You all say some people speak like on the left side of the board. Could they go anywhere and speak that way? Could they go to Harvard?

CLASS: Yes. . . . No.

STOKELY: Does Mr. Turnbow speak like on the left side?

CLASS: Yes.

STOKELY: Could Mr. Turnbow go to Harvard and speak like that? "I wants to reddish to vote."

CLASS: Yes.

STOKELY: Would he be embarrassed?

CLASS: Yes. . . . No!

ZELMA: He wouldn't be, but I would. It doesn't sound right.

STOKELY: Suppose someone from Harvard came to Holmes County and said, "I want to register to vote?" Would they be embarrassed?

ZELMA: No.

STOKELY: Is it embarrassing at Harvard but not in Holmes County? The way you speak?

(p. 5)

The class stopped soon after for lunch, but not before Stokely asked the students to think about what constitutes a society and who makes the rules for society. Students noted that although most people spoke some form of "incorrect English," the "correct English" minority had a monopoly on jobs, money, and prestige. They left wrestling with important questions about language, culture, control, politics, and power. In this brief time in this class, these students were exposed to education at its best: their teacher treated them with respect and valued their knowledge, insight, and know-how as a starting place for a dialogue of learning; the students' knowledge was extended, connected, and compared as a framework for further discovering and knowing; and the students went away more thoughtful and more powerful than when they arrived.

NOTE

1. The following brief account initially appeared in an article I wrote on the civil rights movement and education, entitled, "We who believe in freedom cannot rest until it's done," in *Harvard Education Review*, 59(4), 520–528.

6

KEEPING TRACK

The root of the word "evaluation" is "value," and authentic assessment includes understanding first what students value and then building from there. Authentic assessment is inside-out rather than outside-in. It is an attempt to get away from sorting a mass of students and closer to the teacher's question: Given what I know now, how should I teach this particular student?

When Zayd was in the third grade at P.S. 84, he took his first standardized test. He had told us that there would be no reading, no art, no gym, nothing of the usual routine in the upcoming week—"We're going to be tested," he said with awe. When I asked what it meant "to be tested," he said, "I think we just tell the people what they want to know." Pretty close. He understood that this was an important ritual he must endure, but not much beyond that.

I had spent much of my professional life criticizing standardized tests. I knew that they were biased in hundreds of important ways, that they measured the narrowest band of cognition, and that they did even that rather crudely. I held—and still hold—standardized tests in low regard.

And so I surprised myself when Zayd came home one day several weeks later with the news that he could read at "grade level 8.6." "How wonderful," I immediately thought, "and how insightful of those testers to see how brilliant he is." It was short-lived, but it brought into sharp focus the power standardized tests exert on us all.

A friend of mine—a scholar from Northwestern University—tells the same story from the other side. He was also a critic of standardized tests, and much of his research demonstrated the inadequacy of these tests for assessing the complex growth and development of youngsters. Still, when one of his own kids came home with her test scores down in the basement, he organized the entire world of Northwestern—special diagnostic people, reading and math tutors, test writers—to help his child bring her scores up. "I'm not crazy," he told me, "those scores are like a union card. The union may be crooked and run by gangsters, but, hey, no union card, no work." Again, the power of standardized tests in the lives of students and their families, teachers and principals, cannot be easily dismissed.

The most recent standardized test I took was the basic skills test for a teaching certificate. A huge auditorium was filled with aspirants on the appointed day (we were one of dozens of testing sites throughout the state), each armed with a bachelor's or graduate degree in teaching and a fistful of number two pencils. Precise directions were read aloud twice, and efficient-looking monitors patrolled the hall prepared to escort us to the bathroom, sharpen our pencils, or seize our test booklets if we cheated in any way. This was high ritual.

Two thoughts filled my head as I mindlessly checked off the answers. First was the thought that whatever it was they were testing for, it had no relation to what I understood teaching to be. I might get a perfect score or I might fail the test outright, but neither result would be helpful in determining whether I would succeed or not, whether I would be a good or a rotten teacher. I was asked to divide up the cost of a field trip, for example, to see how much money each child should bring, and I was asked to guess the state capital of Illinois from a list of four cities (Chicago, Springfield, Lincoln, Rockford). Partly, I kept thinking "How idiotic!," "How stupid!," but I was also becoming enraged with some powerful hidden messages in the experience. This test, after all, was the final hurdle to becoming a teacher for thousands of people, and so it fed back for us all of our preparation, summed up the intellectual tradition, and pointed us to a lifetime in teaching. This was our medical boards, after all, our bar exam—the big challenge we would have to meet in order to be found worthy. And it was nothing but simple-minded math, a few facts about history and civics, and a bit of grammar and spelling. Teaching never seemed so silly, so empty, so worthless. And yet, according to the state, if I passed the test, I would now be qualified and ready to teach. That part of the experience made me furious.

The second thought that occupied my mind as I rather mechanically walked through the test grew more slowly and was even more intensely critical; I kept thinking that the test was doing nothing more nor less than checking on my background. The test was dominated by multiple-guess questions in which we were asked to pick the correct sentence from four choices. The question might be set up by asking us to select the correct pronoun-object agreement, or the correct noun-verb agreement. Four sentences would follow:

1. We are going to dinner later.
2. We have going to dinner tomorrow.
3. We be going to dinner this afternoon.
4. We will going to dinner after work.

OR

1. Jim and John fights over the blocks.
2. Jim and John fighting over the blocks.
3. Jim and John fighted over the blocks.
4. Jim and John fought over the blocks.

The fact is that I don't have to pause for one second to figure out what they mean by pronoun object or noun-verb agreement. I grew up in a home where we spoke the exact language being tested for, and so I checked one in the first list and four in the second list without any thought whatsoever. If, on the other hand, I had grown up speaking another language or dialect, say standard Black English, I would likely struggle with the first set of examples. Answers two and four are obviously gibberish, but choice three is more difficult— it is correct Black English and could confound those who speak both conventional and Black English. I can't believe this option is arbitrarily included—it is too specific in who it targets. Similarly, the second set requires years of experience with irregular verbs (Chesa reported recently that he fighted in school—he's only spoken English for ten years), and choice three is the kind of logical extension that would be bewildering, say, to a native Spanish speaker who may be skilled, intelligent, and able in every way. Again, choice three seems designed to hurt specific people. The test was stupid and it was demeaning both to teaching and to the test-takers. It was pretentious and pious in form, but the content was watery and in some ways malevolent. It made teaching mindless and weak, and it was racist in fact if not in intent. I wondered how my fellow test-takers were feeling, and worried about those who would be seduced into seeing this test as somehow a measure of themselves, of teaching, or of both.

I suspect that students taking all kinds of standardized tests have parallel experiences. Tests are surrounded by rituals that underline their central importance. They are also shrouded in secrecy—no one really knows who those folks are in Iowa or wherever, or how they figure out what's important to know. The mystery creates the mystique. And yet taking the test is senseless. Once, when Malik was telling me about his week of standardized testing, I asked, "Did you learn anything from it?" He looked at me with mild disgust. "Bill," he said patronizingly, "it was a test."

Some students must be slightly amused and critical: If this is intelligence or achievement, who cares? Others have their sense of what matters and what counts subtly or profoundly shaped by the experience. After all, standardized tests can't measure initiative, creativity, imagination, conceptual thinking, curiosity, effort, irony, judgment, commitment, nuance, good will, ethical reflection, or a host of other valuable dispositions and attributes. What they can measure and count are isolated skills, specific facts and functions, the least interesting and least significant aspects of learning. And yet, it is hard not to assume that since this is what "counts," this must be knowledge. It is astonishing how easily we are made into rats learning to run any maze put before us.

Breaking the grip of standardized tests requires in part exploding the myth of scientific objectivity that cloaks them. Teachers, parents, and youngsters need to know exactly how the tests are made, who makes them and for what purposes, and who wins and who loses among test-takers. Without this knowledge, our awe of the power of test scores is a bit like the folks admiring the emperor's new clothes—everybody else sees it, so it must be there. Armed with detailed knowledge of the process and the product, we may become like the little boy who can't see the clothes, or at least we will be able to make wise testing decisions within our own educational communities.

Standardized tests are plagued with inherent and intractable problems. This helps explain the army of lawyers and public relations people employed by the big testing companies to keep test sales moving. Standardized tests are culturally biased. That is, they distort the performance of people who are culturally or linguistically different, regardless of ability, intelligence, or achievement. I recently saw an example in a reading test for first graders. There was a pencil sketch of a house with people sitting on the porch, and students were to choose a word to complete the sentence, "The people are sitting on the _____." The choices were, "porch," "ground," "street," "floor." Lots of first-graders I know would be able to read that sentence perfectly well, but would have no idea what a porch is, having never encountered one in their experience and therefore having no occasion to talk or think about it. In time they will find porches (and berms, and saunas, and sushi bars, and many other things) in their lives or in their reading, and their experience and knowledge will grow. But to claim, as this test did, that the question reveals anything profound or essential about reading ability is a sham.

Assume a different cultural stance. Say there is a pencil sketch of tall rectangular buildings crowded together, and youngsters are to

complete this sentence: "Many people live in _____ _____."
The choices are "trees," "forts," "inside," and "projects." Most kids
I know realize that lots of people, including many of them, live in
projects, and so they will answer this question correctly. I suspect that
children in parts of Iowa who could read this would think that a project is something you do with construction paper in school, and so
would guess "forts" as improbable, but the best available answer.

The reporting of test scores is also a sham. Perhaps the most pervasive phrase in the educational idiom is "grade-level." Textbook writers assign numbers arbitrarily to a basal series and everyone acts as if
this book is in some serious way linked to the fourth grade. Or test
makers report a child's score as a year below (or above) grade-level,
and there is general panic (or joy). Grade-level equivalency is part of
the common sense of schooling, officially sanctioned and popularly
accepted.

But it is not very well understood. This is how it works: If a fifth
grade girl, for example, receives a grade-level score of 5.7 on a reading
test, that simply means that on a particular day, when a particular test
was given, she got a certain number of answers correct—in this case,
she got the same number correct as the student who achieved the
median score when the test was first tried out—that is, the middle
score of all those fifth-graders ranked in a sample given in some previ-
ous year in March (5 means the fifth grade, 7 is the seventh month
of the school year). The scores are figured by giving a small sample of
fifth graders a test, and then spreading their scores out along a continuum. The middle score from the sample group stands as the norm,
and grade-level equivalents are worked out up and down the scale
from that point. There is no real link, however, between 4.2 or 6.9
and fourth graders or sixth graders in this example, because no fourth
graders or sixth graders ever took the test. Furthermore, by the nature
of how these tests are constructed, it is impossible for all students to
be on grade level—that would be like having all the teams in the
National League playing above .500. So while a sensible school goal
might be for all third graders to be competent and capable of reading
a wide range of materials for a broad variety of purposes, from a testing point of view the goal is to sort scores along a continuum.

Sorting children into winners and losers is the main business of
the standardized tests. And the tragedy is that we know before the
tests are even administered who is going to land where. The single
most powerful predictor of how a child will do on any standardized
test is how he or she did on the first test ever taken; and the single
most powerful predictor of how a child will do on that first test is the

economic status and educational background of the parents. We really need to rethink the value of this expensive, time-consuming, authoritarian enterprise if what it mainly tells us is something we could find out by simply asking: "How much money does your mom make? . . . OK, you're on the bottom." This may seem far-fetched, but the testing business really does push our schools toward becoming this kind of elaborate sorting machine. If we want something different, we need to seriously rework certain priorities.

Standardized tests push well-intentioned teachers and school leaders in the wrong direction; they constrain teachers' energies and minds, dictating a disastrously narrow range of activities and experiences, and offering little help in the important job of figuring out where kids are in order to present the next challenge. For example, if young children are to have a strong experiential base for future success in math and reading, they need many opportunities to work with blocks and puzzles, to paint and play games, to explore a wide range of books, to have stories read to them and to write in journals or diaries. The problem is that none of this will yield quick results on a multiple-choice test, none of it will show up in the "right way" or on time. And so a curriculum of work sheets and drill and skill replaces all that is most needed.

This problem is intensified for students who do poorly on these kinds of tests. While well-intentioned school people may want these youngsters to succeed, and may work feverishly in many cases to prepare them for the tests, these children are too often lacking what their privileged counterparts already have: exposure to real books, conversations about the content of stories, a word-rich and literate environment, and an understanding of the power of language and the pleasures and rewards of reading. By focusing on the ability to answer multiple-choice questions, reading is reduced to a set of relatively unimportant skills, and the link between reading and power is further broken. Test scores stay low, and once again, those who need the most get the least.

I assume that bad tests are worse than no tests at all. Standardized tests are bad tests. Instead of encouraging youngsters and bringing them into a community of learners, tests drive students away. Tests feel arbitrary and hollow, even to those who succeed at them. They do not loop back to learning or teaching in any important or even apparent way and, therefore, they are largely meaningless for teachers struggling to teach. If tests were at any time embedded in a context linked to teaching and learning, that context has been lost, and tests now add to a profound sense that schooling is without authentic

value. Standardized tests should come with printed warnings: USE OF
THESE MATERIALS MAY BE HAZARDOUS TO YOUR INTELLIGENCE, or,
THE LIFE CHANCES OF HALF OF THOSE TAKING THESE TESTS WILL
BE NARROWED.

Courageous school principles and school district leaders require
standardized tests only when absolutely necessary to comply with state
law. In Illinois, this means only in the third, sixth, eighth, and eleventh
grades. Sensible school districts around the nation have banned
K–2 standardized testing. This is not enough.

Teachers, schools, and school districts can refuse to buy into the
testing mystique, even if they are required by some higher authority
to administer tests, even when they are in some sense accountable for
results. One creative way to do this is for teachers to go ahead and
develop with children the kind of environment for learning, curriculum,
and program that best suits their youngsters, and to allow this
approach to guide teaching from September through March. A few
weeks before T-Day, teachers could meet with students (in a group
and individually) and explain the facts of testing. They might talk
openly about cultural bias, they might explain how test results automatically
hurt half the kids, they might describe some of what these
tests cannot measure. Students might develop a little project, analyzing
past test questions, figuring out how one computes grade-level
equivalencies or "stanines," looking at the debate swirling around
standardized tests, and so on. Teachers would certainly explain to students
that reading (all the exciting and valuable work we've been doing)
is not the same as test-taking.

In short, teachers would tell the truth about standardized tests,
they would stop pretending that tests are sanctified, agreed-on, god-given
texts, and they would invite students into an important discussion
that has direct bearing on their lives and from which they have
been excluded. They would then proceed—coldly, determinedly,
straightforwardly—to teach test-taking, that is, how to read short
pieces, guess at answers, deduce the biases of test-makers, and so on.
This is largely what the expensive cram courses offered to middle class
youngsters do. I think it's only fair for teachers to provide it to all
students.

Another way to resist the tests even as one participates in them is
to fight to bring them into some meaningful perspective. If the only
tool you have is a hammer, then you tend to treat everything like a
nail; developing and using a wider range of tools is a way to stop
hammering everyone. For example, students and teachers can determine
a whole range of "products" that will be developed in the course

of a school year, and test results will be one of those products. College admissions officers are increasingly open to this approach, and whether college-bound or not, all youngsters deserve an opportunity to mark their development and plot a future. If test results are tucked into a portfolio that includes, say, an autobiography, a written analysis of a work of art that moved the student, a map of the neighborhood with proposed improvements, a sonnet, a record of community service, a discussion of an ethical value that the student attempted to embody in a real-life situation, a board game the student invented, a description of some physical challenge the student attempted, an original song, a reflection on a current international event and its implications locally, an artifact made of wood by the student, a plan for what the student wants to accomplish in the future, and so on—test results would be brought down to scale. Standing alone, as the only record of a student's school life, test results loom too large—they take on a meaning they do not deserve.

———

Alternatives to standardized tests can be thought of as the three p's: projects, portfolios, and performance. These are attempts to keep assessment authentic, that is, to assess students in the real contexts of their lives. Authentic assessment strategies move away from tests that stand as surrogates for the real world and assume that the real world matters. Instead of reading a disconnected paragraph, for example, youngsters might read an entire story and discuss it with a teacher; instead of multiple-choice questions standing for skill in reading or writing, students might write original essays. These assessment strategies yield a richer kind of evaluation, more sensitive to differences, more complex, more useful to teachers, more rooted in reality, more authentic.

Of course, this approach is more student-centered, too, and more teacher-friendly, and it is easy to see its value "one to one to one," one classroom at a time. It is difficult to imagine a "national, standardized, authentic test," and yet, as grass-roots interest in alternatives to standardized testing grows, that is precisely what the big testing companies are trying to develop. It is a project doomed to fail. First, moving authentic assessment away from specific teachers in specific classrooms removes the authenticity from it and undermines its usefulness. Authentic assessment must be continuous, and it must account for and accommodate a broad range of dynamic interests and abilities. Authentic assessment is properly in the service of student learning and in the hands of teachers making concrete teaching decisions in actual contexts. Without this rich and deep context, and without this control, it loses its heart. It becomes the same old brutal standardized testing with a new name and a modern facade.

Second, it is simply too expensive. The testing industry already consumes millions and millions of educational dollars; it is estimated that developing national written and performance-based tests would cost up to ten times what we are now spending. Is this where our educational resources should go?

Finally, there is an inherent danger in developing a single national standard in a complex and diverse democracy. Giving a small group— no matter how professional, no matter how well-intentioned—the right to set a standard for all is totalitarian. Those technicians and professionals who advocate a national standard now assume that their standard will carry the day. If some other small but powerful group established a single standard, those same professionals would lead the rebellion. It is wiser and more hopeful to keep decisions about values and standards closer to parents, communities, children, and teachers. This means that it can be difficult to compare across communities sometimes, but it maintains an essential freedom too—the freedom to choose what is valuable, the freedom to establish standards for oneself, one's community, and one's children.

In order to assess or evaluate anything or anyone, we must begin by knowing what we value. This helps explain my difficulty with taking standardized test scores too seriously (except in regard to narrowing life chances, which I think is a deadly serious business)—I simply don't value very much the ability to identify pieces of information or perform mechanical functions. Beginning with what we value offers a hopeful entry point into the area of testing, assessment, and evaluation.

When we hold up a standard, what we are saying, in effect, is, "Here is what we value." I believe schools should uphold high standards for all youngsters, and that those standards should be available, accessible, and understood by all. The development of standards should, in fact, be fundamental work for every school and for each classroom, because developing standards is a critical way to bring people together with a focus on core concerns. This can take a lot of time and energy, but it will be useful and well-spent energy if it results in standards that are understood and embraced by all. When new parents or students come into the community, or when anyone disagrees with the established standards, the dialogue simply continues and perhaps even deepens—people can defend the existing standards or change them to reflect their own developing perspectives. The point is that if we want to build a thoughtful educational community of youngsters, parents, and teachers, standards must be internal, accessible, and defensible. The child and the classroom must be the center of knowledge about classrooms and children, and assessment must serve the work at hand. This sense of standards should not be confused with "standardized"—the process of narrowing, punishing, and controlling from the outside that too often passes for assessment.

Breaking with the notion that a grade-level equivalent is a useful standard, I want teachers to search elsewhere. Teachers can investigate, for example, what kind of standards children have. What do they expect of us, what standard do they uphold in relation to us as teachers? ("Teachers should be fair."; "Teachers should be strict but nice.") Or what standard do they uphold in regard to themselves and reading? Or what standard do they uphold for justice? ("My mom says if anyone touches me, I've got to kick their ass.") Finding out helps us become better teachers. All of it matters.

It is further helpful to start from an assumption that all youngsters are struggling to make sense of the world. This is common ground, and helps us remember that all children are in some way productive and valuable, that they are all (given everything) doing the best they can, and that they are all themselves potentially people of values. The question for teachers then becomes, what is this child striving for, what is he trying to make sense of, where are her standards? If we can recognize the child, uncover her sense-making journey, reveal her standards (to her, to ourselves), we will have unlocked a large space for keeping track of growth and learning.

Even in the context of specific classes or subjects, standards should not be associated with ideas that are represented by phrases like, "You must learn this bit of stuff in this way and at this time or you will fail." For example, asking youngsters to write a descriptive essay, a critical review, a plot summary or a character sketch, all have standards embedded in them. Upholding these standards implies even broader standards: the ability to read critically and for enjoyment, the ability to communicate with others through many media, and so on. And again, broad standards that a class, or a group of youngsters, or a cohort are working to uphold are quite different from what standardized tests require and assume.

―――――――

Besides a lot of informal assessment of each child, teachers need more formal ways to keep track of themselves, their work, and each child's purposes, investments, growth, and needs. This is especially true in situations where classes are too big, where teachers are buried in too much paperwork, where test scores, grades, and standardized ways of looking at youngsters dominate, and where teachers don't have regular and formal opportunities to discuss their work with one another. It is these imperfect settings that demand even more effort by teachers to work toward their own systems of authentic assessment.

Structuring into the school routine opportunities for projects, performances, and portfolios is a beginning. This allows teachers to see what students are up to while asking them to do the work themselves. Regular oral reports, enactments, productions, constructions, creations—all of these and more put student work on display, and allow teachers to assess work in the regular rhythm of classroom life. Portfolios are an additional way of making standards, goals, and values clear. For example, in my seminar for teachers we discuss classroom issues regularly, we work on a wide variety of complex concerns, and we range over a lot of densely covered ground. And in the end, each student presents a portfolio that includes: a learning agenda, a pedagogical autobiography, a description of core teaching values, a letter to the author of a self-selected, published teacher autobiography, a child study, a brief philosophy of education, a self-evaluation, a recollection of outstanding moments as a student, a description of a failed teaching attempt, a review of a self-selected autobiography of childhood, a practical art, and a revised learning agenda or action plan for the immediate future. This portfolio leaves a lot out, of course, but it also reflects and emphasizes qualities I value in teaching.

While there is no system that is right for all teachers and all students at all times, keeping track requires an investment of energy and time to reflect, write, and gather materials. Here is a menu of possibilities:

- *Student work.* Many teachers keep a file cabinet or a shelf or a special space to collect and preserve student work. This becomes an archive and a museum of student effort and progress.
- *Checklists.* Some teachers create easy checklists that will encourage quick note-taking in the course of the day. One checklist might have regular activities listed and space to jot in names.
- *Tape recorders.* Others find it convenient to take "notes" with a recorder either during the day, or traveling to and from school.
- *Anecdotal records.* A few teachers take the time to write a running anecdotal account of the behavior of a specific child during project time or free time. Teachers try to shadow a child with-

out dogging him, and these anecdotal records are traces of children at work, a chronicle of student progress.

- *Time samples.* Sometimes teachers make a point of jotting down
  what children are doing in five-minute intervals, again creating
  a trail over time of children's choices and behaviors.
- *Journals.* Teachers may find journals or diaries essential partners
  in a reflective dialogue on teaching, providing the necessary audience for a thoughtful conversation.
- *Child observation.* Besides reflective journals, some teachers set
  a goal of writing about specific students at the end of each
  week, say, everything they can think of about five students. In
  six weeks they've got evidence of something on every student
  in the class. A path is being mapped.
- *Partners/mentors.* Many teachers seek out one other teacher—a
  friend, ally, or senior colleague—and set up a regular meeting
  time to discuss children and teaching.
- *Support groups.* Teachers' support groups provide a larger fo-
  rum for challenge and support. Some support groups focus on
  teaching problems, others on advocacy, and others on thinking
  about children's learning.

All of these options provide opportunities for teachers to keep track
of their own teaching, to go back and analyze, to collect valuable data
and information, to see if any students are being missed, and to assess
success. They provide the necessary signposts for each child's unique
passage.

Herb Zimiles (1987) argues that standardized achievement tests are
problematic, in part because of their "exaggerated importance, the
false validity that is imputed to evaluation data, the aura of definitive-
ness that they cast (even when evaluators are modest in their claims),
and the tangled web of comparisons and wrong inferences they invite"
(p. 207). He further highlights:

> . . . [the] serious limitations associated with the low validity of the find-
> ings of educational evaluation (and when I speak of low validity I refer
> to both inaccuracy in measurement and, to a greater extent, irrelevance
> of measurement) and the pressures that evaluation programs implicitly
> bring to bear on teachers, pressures that impel them to use methods and
> to teach content that may not fit in with their vision of what would most
> benefit the children in their class (or worse, materials that discourage

them from ever having a vision of the educational process that differs from that which is implicitly stated in evaluation programs), thereby impair- the depth, coherence, and power of their work. (p. 209)

Zimiles believes that "since we are unable to accurately assess the main lines of school influence, we should instead direct our evaluation efforts to assessing the quality of the school environment" (p. 210). Providing thick descriptions of the character and kinds of environments children are exposed to provides a reasonable basis to "estimate the quality of school impact" (p. 210).

In all of this, we are in pursuit of the child's pathway to knowledge and power. The more recognizable and well-defined our standards—our values—the more manifest and discernible can be student progress. There are all kinds of ways to keep track, but the most hopeful approaches are those that encourage multiple routes to a goal, and a diversity of powerful voices and choices.

7

THE MYSTERY
OF TEACHING

The work of a teacher—exhausting, complex, idiosyncratic, never twice the same—is, at its heart, an intellectual and ethical enterprise. Teaching is the vocation of vocations, a calling that shepherds a multitude of other callings. It is an activity that is intensely practical and yet transcendent, brutally matter-of-fact, and yet fundamentally a creative act. Teaching begins in challenge and is never far from mystery.

Teaching is highly personal—an intensely intimate encounter. The rhythm of teaching involves a complex journey, a journey of discovery and wonder, disappointment and fulfillment. A first step is becoming the student to your students; uncovering the fellow creatures who must be partners to the enterprise. Another is creating an environment for learning, a nurturing and challenging space in which to travel. And finally, the teacher must begin work on the intricate, many-tiered bridges that will fill up the space, connecting all the dreams, hopes, skills, experiences, and knowledge students bring to class with deeper and wider ways of knowing. Teaching requires a vast range of knowledge, ability, skill, judgment, and understanding—and it requires a thoughtful, caring person at its center.

Teaching is not something one learns to do, once and for all, and then practices, problem-free, for a lifetime, anymore than one knows how to have friends, and follows a static set of directions called "friendships" through each encounter. Teaching depends on growth and development, and it is practiced in dynamic situations that are never twice the same. Wonderful teachers, young and old, will tell of fascinating insights, new understandings, unique encounters with youngsters, the intellectual puzzle and the ethical dilemmas that provide a daily challenge. Teachers, above all, must stay alive and engaged with all of this.

We are in a sense back at the beginning. It is perhaps even clearer that teaching involves a dazzling array of activities and experiences, a blizzard of actions and reactions, an attic-full of knowledge and skill. This is in part why I marvel at academics and policy-makers who so glibly prescribe for teachers, who provide tidy summaries on how to teach, who offer the "magic bullet" for instant classroom success, or who pursue projects that will finally capture and tame teaching into a set of neat propositions. I wish I knew only one thing about teaching as well as they seem to know everything. There are, in fact, a range of important skills and experiences needed to become an outstanding teacher—skills rarely acknowledged in colleges of education and never mentioned in schools. These are the subversive core of excellent teaching.

Stanislavsky (1936), the renowned Russian director and the father of method acting, argues that there are three widespread, common beliefs about acting that stand in the way of greatness. One is the belief that acting is a set of techniques and directions to be mastered. In other words, if you say your lines, move to the appointed spot on the stage, complete a specified gesture, then you are acting. Stanislavsky dismissed this as mechanical nonsense. Plenty of people can memorize lines and move around a stage, but great actors engage an audience, interact with them, and draw energy and inspiration from the relationship. Acting is dynamic.

A second obstacle is the notion that acting is mainly external. That is, you can act angry without ever having felt anger, or you can play a broken-hearted lover without ever knowing pain or loss. For Stanislavsky, actors must reach inside themselves and summon up particular aspects of their own knowledge and experience in order to act. Actors must be autobiographers, must in some sense play themselves, must find somewhere a seed of authenticity to build on. Only then can they move away from simple caricatures and learn to portray the complexities of living, human beings.

Finally, a barrier to great acting is the view that actors should, or even could learn their roles in some summative or final sense. In other words, once an actor's got Lady Macbeth, it is "hers." Stanislavsky argues that as soon as an actor believes she or he is master of the part, rigor mortis is already setting in. Being finished denies the uniqueness of each encounter with the character, destroys the dynamic and the creative core of acting. Any part must be learned anew, day by day, moment by moment, and year by year. It is never done. In essence, great acting is always in search of better acting, always beginning again.

Stanislavsky could well be advising teachers. Greatness in teaching, too, requires a serious encounter with autobiography: Who are you? How did you come to take on your views and outlooks? What forces helped to shape you? What was it like for you to be ten? What have you made of yourself? Where are you heading? An encounter with these kinds of questions is critical to outstanding teaching because teachers, whatever else they teach, teach themselves. Of all the knowledge teachers need to draw on, self-knowledge is most important (and least attended to). In this regard Rilke's (1934) advice to a young poet is appropriate:

> You are looking outward and that above all you should not do now. . . .
> There is only one single way. Go into yourself. Search for the reason that
> bids you write [or teach], find out whether it is spreading out its roots
> in the deepest places of your heart.

Greatness in teaching also requires getting over the notion that teaching is a set of techniques or disconnected methods. There are lots of people who write adequate lesson plans, keep order and quiet in their classrooms, deliver competent instruction in algebra or phonics, and are lousy teachers. Outstanding teachers engage youngsters, interact with them, draw energy and direction from them, and find ways to give them a reason to follow along. This is the difficult and serious work of teaching.

Greatness in teaching, as in acting or writing, is always in pursuit of the next utterance, the next performance, the next encounter. It is not—can never be—finished or summed up. Keeping track is in service of what is yet to come. Great teaching demands an openness to something new, something unique, something dynamic. In teaching it must always be, "Here I go again."

There are hundreds of other things one needs to know to become an outstanding teacher, many of which teachers will discover as they are needed. Here is a small sample:

• *Creative insubordination.* I had been teaching at P.S. 269 for about four hours when the intercom squawked on for the seventh time: "If anyone drives a red station wagon, your lights are on." The seventh mindless interruption (the first had been a scratchy recording of the "Star Spangled Banner"); the seventh assault on our senses; the seventh reminder that our space was not our own and that learning was not respected. I got a screwdriver, pulled a table over to the wall, took apart the intercom, clipped the wires, and reassembled the whole thing. I then sent a student to the office with the bad news that our intercom was dysfunctional. It took three years to repair—three years of liberation from the box.

Every successful teacher I know (and every principal) can tell stories of creative insubordination—of regulations ignored, paper work "lost," procedures subverted. An enormous number of the existing regulations in schools serve bureaucracy but not youngsters. The guiding principle is simple: creative insubordination is justified if it serves student learning.

• *Criticism/self-criticism.* In the lunch room at P.S. 269 a colleague reprimanded a misbehaving seven-year-old girl by brandishing a pair of scissors and threatening to cut off her pony tail. I intervened, comforted the child, and pursued a complaint against him through an incredible wall of pressure to back down. It was unpleasant, but it opened an important conversation about appropriate and inappropriate discipline, about humiliation and abuse versus concern and community.

If teachers are never critical, they never have to test their deepest beliefs and values, and over time those values disappear. Soon they are acting like the teachers they once despised, they have become the people they once warned others about, and they have forgotten all the things that made them want to teach in the first place.

Similarly, if teachers are never self-critical they will lose their capacity for renewal and growth. They will become self-justifying and dogmatic. On the other side, if teachers are too self-critical they become powerless and timid. The tension is to end each day with a strong understanding of what could be improved, and to begin the next with forgiveness and hope.

Teachers are taught, in all kinds of ways, lessons in accommodation and conformity when they ought to be learning criticism and self-criticism. Teachers need to be critical because so much of schooling is inadequate or wrong; self-critical because there is always a new challenge, a new demand. Learning to be critical requires taking some risks, and these are neither simple nor easy to take. Again, the guiding principle is to be a resistance fighter on behalf of children, not to take risks simply to stay in shape.

• *Finding allies.* Teaching is often isolated and isolating, and an assumption of teacher preparation is that it must always be this way.

In fact, outstanding teaching is usually teaching against the grain, and teaching against the grain can best be accomplished with allies. This means supporters, friends, co-conspirators, and comrades. Learning how to find allies and build alliances can be life-saving.

• *Learning from your own experience.* When we sent our first child off to school I experienced a jarring moment, an epiphany. I had been teaching young children for many years, advising parents on a wide range of issues, including the best and most painless ways to separate from their youngsters at school. When my own time came, I found that all my good advice to others was impossible to follow myself. Separation was tough. I felt like a midwife friend of mine who had assisted in the births of hundreds of babies before her own first child was born. In the middle of labor she cried out, "I've told hundreds of women, 'you can do it,' and it can't be done."

Teachers are encouraged to develop a professional stance that is outside their own experience. They are expected to assume a distanced superiority and to speak an arcane and inaccessible language. It is stronger and more fruitful to practice humility in the classroom, to have the courage to admit what you don't know, to invite others to teach you, and to stay close to your own experience. Good teaching requires audacity, but it also demands humility.

• *Linking consciousness to conduct.* It is important to be both a dreamer and a doer, to hold onto ideals but also to struggle continually to enact those ideals in concrete situations. Many teachers begin with a romanticized idea of a "peaceable kingdom in the classroom," rather than a robust, interactive, dynamic space. They harbor the illusion that the classroom can be easily walled off from larger issues in the children's (and all of our) lives, and that their own good intentions will be enough to make their classrooms places of sweetness and light. When the classroom proves to be somewhat unpredictable, when issues from "out there" become enacted "in here," when teaching is more exhausting, demanding, and uncertain than ever imagined, teachers can become frustrated, disillusioned, and burned out.

The way out, I believe, is to expect that teaching in a humane, child-centered way is not easier but requires greater intelligence, reflection, justification, and commitment. It is teaching toward something better, and it requires, therefore, involvement in the wider world of children and families, of communities and neighborhoods, of society. Holding onto ideals is a way to resist acceding to the unacceptable things we find in the world; struggling alongside others to improve society is a way to become more focused and more effective as teachers, and also as citizens.

• *Authentic friendship.* The ideal of friendship can be a guide for teaching, or it can be a trap. Teachers who start off desperately wanting to be "friends" with their students often end up being distant, authoritarian, and arbitrary, in part because they thought of friendship as a matter of being likable, popular, or nice. With this somewhat surface notion of friendship, it is easy to become inappropriate with students, to lose your bearings, or to become confused about how to act. Feeling betrayed, friends can turn easily into enemies.

One student teacher I worked with spoke openly about his living arrangements and sex life when talking with middle school students on the first day in their classroom. They had asked, and he was "being their friend." The incident, needless to say, was a disaster for him and for them. He had failed to really examine what it means to be a friend. Like a new kid on the block, he was prodded and provoked, and his desire to be popular led to his downfall.

A stronger sense of friendship is to think in terms of deep caring and compassion for others. Friendship, then, is a matter of solidarity between subjects, between human beings, and solidarity means criticism as well as acceptance. We share some intimate matters with certain friends, but not all. We don't want our friends doing something we take to be wrong, and so we are willing to raise questions and criticisms, even when that can be difficult. We don't want our friends to be weak or hopeless, and so we are willing to offer guidance and advice. Being popular or being liked every moment is not the point—a real friendship has bumpy and difficult times, too, and that can be the greater part of its strength.

• *Balance and clarity.* There are literally thousands of good ideas floating around for making classrooms more decent and dynamic. The problem is that ideas come at teachers ninety miles an hour, and teachers need to choose what will work for them and their students. Trying to implement a new idea every day is not a particularly hopeful strategy. One problem is that big transformative ideas require sustained attention. "Whole language," for example, if taken seriously, could completely transform school practice, the shape of the day, the meaning of curriculum, everything. "Character education" could mean an entirely different school culture and ethos. If, on the other hand, they are the latest fads, something to fit into existing classroom practice, techniques and nothing more, then teachers can say things like, "We do whole language in ability groups from 9:00–9:30," or, "We do character education after lunch."

Teachers are typically trapped in the role of passive recipients rather than of active creators of their teaching. Teachers can resist this by operating out of the principal of "less is more," deciding what makes sense at the center of their own classroom life, and implementing that central core while resisting all the free-falling, well-meaning ideas. The best staff development, then, is not another workshop with an educational guru, but is visiting classrooms of other teachers you admire, or carving out time and space to reflect seriously on core principles and practices.

Good schools are generally places where a lot of good teachers have been gathered together and allowed to teach. This means school leaders have attracted and recruited good teachers, and then run interference with bureaucratic regulations, state mandates, and the entire apparatus that undermines teaching.

Good schools are always unique: each the creation of particular teachers, administrators, parents, and youngsters working together to bring their vision of a better educational experience to life in classrooms. Good schools do not follow a generic, one-size-fits-all approach to education, but rely instead on a community of people working together, figuring out how to solve problems and improve their school on a daily basis, and then gathering the freedom to act on their conclusions. Reform must be crafted school by school, from the bottom up, and school improvement is generally a matter for the school community itself.

"Goodness" is complex and hard to measure on a simple scale, but there are several themes that, taken together, make a school more likely to be effective. Good schools tend to be organized around and powered by a set of *core values*. Values may be drawn from long tradition or from the specific needs and orientations of particular communities, but they must be embraced and owned by the community itself. Values cannot simply be tacked on, but must be explicit, obvious, and embodied in the daily life of the school.

Good schools have *high expectations for all learners.* The school community has straightforward goals that apply to all students and yet are flexible and personalized for each. They find ways to nurture and challenge the wide range of youngsters who actually arrive at school, and they don't consider the condition of the lives of their students a reasonable excuse for failure.

Good schools are places where *teachers are respected* and are expected to be responsible decision-makers. Teachers are not cogs in a machine, but feel themselves to be valuable, even indispensable. Each teacher feels a sense of authorship of her own teaching text, ownership of her own work.

Good schools are *geared to continuous improvement*. No school, no teaching, no curriculum is ever perfect; good schools are places where people are neither smug nor complacent. Good schools are always in the making.

I have tried to change, create, or improve schools and classrooms for much of my life. One thing I have learned along the way is that there are no guarantees—you dive into the work with faith and hope and fear. Another is that you must think big, question everything, and not merely tinker around the edges—rearranging the deck chairs on the Titanic might make for a more pleasant view, but it does not prevent the inevitable plunge to the ocean floor. At the same time, you must attend to details, to the needs and desires of specific people. You must think globally and act locally, head in the stars and feet on the ground. It's a stretch.

Recently, I have been working with an energetic group of parents and teachers to create a small public school within a large school building. Called the Imani School, this project is still more dream than reality, more faith than substance. *Imani* means "faith" in Swahili—the name was suggested by a teacher who keeps the faith for a brighter future as well as anyone I know.

The community drawn together to build this school is not made up of idle dreamers. Imani School is located in a poor, urban neighborhood. Many of the families live in depressed, dilapidated, and neglected housing projects. Most of the youngsters have witnessed violence firsthand, all are aware of the presence of exploitation and crime. One of the things that makes these teachers and parents so inspiring is precisely their willingness and ability to fight for a decent school and future for their children when there are so many reasons to give up.

An initial focus of the Imani School planning group was to "turn weaknesses into strengths." We organized small teams to tour and map the neighborhood, looking for community assets. The larger challenge was to name the putative problems, and to see if they could be transformed into assets.

The park, fire house, and small commercial district are obvious community strengths. How can the school use them? Classes can take trips, perhaps, or organize a community campaign to keep the park clean. Some classes might "adopt" a restaurant or small business to

study and support. These assets are worth naming, and it is valuable
to figure out how to bring them more fully into the life of the school.

A deeper challenge is to try to look at problems from the other
side. There are several vacant lots near the school—are these potential
sites for gardens or play lots? The community has a high rate of unemployment—can some unemployed adults be organized to work in or
around the school on specific projects? The planning group isn't certain, but attempting to turn weaknesses into strengths has expanded
people's imaginative space.

One thing the group did early on was to try to discover our deep,
collective values. We imagined that each of us had the power to magi-
cally bestow on all the people of the world three qualities, and we
asked ourselves what they would be. These qualities could not be
physical attributes like good health, material goods like wealth or a
Rolls Royce, or specific religious affiliations. But beyond that, they
could be anything at all.

We worked and worked on this activity, individually and in groups,
and eventually achieved consensus on five qualities: compassion, curiosity, respect for others and self, creativity, and an ability to participate
fully in society. This took a long time, and it represented a lot of
conversation, struggle, compromise, and redefinition.

These qualities became for us our core values, a guide to future
action. Since these were qualities we wanted for all people, qualities
that would in some sense improve the world, we felt that they had to
come alive and be readily apparent in school practice. We could not in
good conscience teach the rules of grammar and ignore, for example,
respect. How could curiosity become evident in the hallways? Would
there be respect in the cafeteria? What would it look like? Was compassion going to be a part of every single interaction? How? None of this
solved the problem of what to do in school, but it did provide a helpful lens through which to imagine and examine practice.

These core values led to an emphasis on democracy and active
participation in social life. As one of the parents put it, "We should
act as if we live in a democracy, and in that way make it become more
so." Respect and fairness would be explicitly emphasized in the
school, and teachers would strive to create classrooms where people
can think and question freely, speak and write and read critically, work
cooperatively, consider the common good and then act accordingly.
Every class would need to have community service built into the
day—the youngest children might tend a garden, for example, others
would help in tutoring projects, the oldest would work in community

organizations, and everyone would have to be involved in clean-up and maintenance.

The planning group emphasized the importance of experience as a teacher—hands-on learning, research projects involving first-person encounters and primary sources. There is a commitment from teachers to use the community and its residents as a school resource. Everyone teaches, everyone learns, and knowledge is keyed to action, experimentation, reflection, self-correction, discovery, and surprise. There is a desire to encourage youngsters to write their own stories and plays, to build on what they know and experience even when it is difficult or painful to do so. No student will be silenced.

Of course, developing an education based on experience is just the beginning. John Dewey (1938) noted that experience and education are not the same thing. We are all having experiences all the time, and yet some experiences may be disconnected events leading nowhere, or they may even be uneducative in the sense that they shut down or distort future growth. The challenge for teachers who are building an education based on experience is to create opportunities for students to have the kinds of experiences that will enable them to grow and develop into further experiences, and eventually to take control of their own learning. Allowing youngsters to tell their stories is one hopeful activity; providing them access to a wide range of materials is another. We know we are successful when students are willing to forge their own next steps, when they face the future with some love, some indignation, and a lot of courage.

Students at Imani School will be respected—valued for who they are, and honored for who they are becoming. Their projects, it is hoped, will shape much of the day, and their concrete efforts will keep the place running. Students will know that without them, the lunchroom would not be beautiful, the grounds would not be kept up, and nothing would work. This is in sharp contrast to schools where the very presence of students is seen mainly as a problem, an encumbrance, an obstacle to the smooth functioning of the place. Teachers at Imani School want to communicate a deeply held belief that they value children, that they find their own work meaningful precisely because of the presence and activity of youngsters. The planning group wants there to be neither a cult of youth, nor a cult of adulthood, but rather a sense of intergenerational dependence, care, responsibility, and commitment.

Imani School is being built. It is still in the planning stages, more possibility than reality, and it may not get where it hopes to go. But it seems to me to be on the right track, a project that rejects the notion that school failure is inevitable, and, most importantly, acts in common purpose with parents and youngsters. No one at Imani is "saving children"—we are saving one another, and, perhaps with enough faith in people, saving the future.

———————

Frederick Douglass tells a remarkable story of learning to read as a subversive activity. As a slave, Douglass had no rights and meager opportunities. Reading among slaves was strictly forbidden for it could open worlds and create unimaginable mischief. Besides, according to their overlords, slaves had no need of reading. They could be trained in the necessary menial and backbreaking work. Yet his master's wife, believing him to be an intelligent youngster, undertook to teach Douglass how to read the Bible in hopes that he would come closer to God. When the master discovered the crime, he exploded: "It will unfit him to be a slave!"

Education will unfit anyone to be a slave. That is because education is bold, adventurous, creative, vivid, illuminating—in other words, education is for self-activating explorers of life, for those who would challenge fate, for doers and activists, for citizens. Training is for slaves, for loyal subjects, for tractable employees, for willing consumers, for obedient soldiers. Education tears down walls; training is all barbed wire.

What we call education is usually no more than training. We are so busy operating schools that we have lost sight of learning. We mostly participate in certification mills, institutions founded on notions of control and discipline, lifeless and joyless places where people serve time and master a few basic skills on their way to a plain piece of paper that justifies and sanctions the whole affair. Sometimes, these places are merely mindless, and sometimes they are expressly malevolent.

A hundred years ago, this country developed a system of schools run out of the Interior Department called Indian Boarding Schools, a few of which survive to this day. The premise of these schools is that Native American children can be educated if they are stripped of everything Indian and taught to be like whites. Taken from their homes, these youngsters were punished severely for speaking their own languages, practicing their own religions, or attempting to contact their families. Everything Native had to be erased as a first step toward official learning. Some students, of course, went along, but many rebelled, refused to learn, and were labeled intractable.

The cost of education at an Indian Boarding School was great—dignity, individuality, humanity, maybe even sanity. The payoff was rather small: a menial job, a marginal place in the social order. Students had to submit to humiliation, degradation, and mutilation simply to learn how to function at the lowest levels of society. No wonder most refused: The price was high, the benefit meager.

It is not much different in many schools today. We claim to be giving students key skills and knowledge, and yet we deny them the one thing that is essential to their survival: something to live for. All the units in drug awareness, gang prevention, and mental health together are not worth that single hopeful thing.

When we as teachers recognize that we are partners with our students in life's long and complex journey, when we begin to treat them with the dignity and respect they deserve for simply being, then we are on the road to becoming worthy teachers. It is just that simple—and just that difficult.

Jane Addams, founder of Hull House, once asked, "How shall we respond to the dreams of youth?" It is a dazzling and elegant question, a question that demands an answer—a range of answers, really, spiraling outward in widening circles. It is a teacher's kind of question. It is a question to take with us as we plunge into teaching, full of dread and hope, alive to both, living a teacher's life, singular and mysterious, helping to create a generation unfit for slavery.

8

BEGINNING AGAIN: THE CURRENT CHALLENGE TO TEACH

"If I only had a home . . . a heart . . . a brain . . . the nerve."

The four hopeful seekers skipping together down the yellow brick road toward Oz sing their desires to one another and to the heavens. Each has diagnosed a deficiency, identified a lack, recognized a need. Each has become painfully conscious of something missing, a hole in need of repair. Each is stirred to action against an obstacle to his or her fullness, and each gathers momentum and power from the others, from intimate relationship forged through collective struggle.

This is not a bad start for teachers seeking a vocabulary of basic qualities in their quest for wholeness and for goodness in teaching—a home, a heart, a brain, the nerve. There is more, to be sure, but these can send you skipping down your own yellow brick roads into the wide, wide world beyond.

Teaching is intellectual and ethical work; it takes a thoughtful, reflective, and caring person to do it well. It takes a brain and a heart. The first and fundamental challenge for teachers is to embrace students as three-dimensional creatures, as distinct human beings with hearts and minds and skills and dreams and capacities of their own, as people much like ourselves. This embrace is initially an act of faith—we must assume capacity even when it is not immediately apparent or visible, we must hew to "the substance of things hoped for, the evidence of things unseen"—because we work most often in schools where aggregating and grouping kids on the flimsiest evidence is the reigning common-sense, where the toxic habit of labeling youngsters on the basis of their deficits is a common place. A teacher needs a brain to break through the cotton wool smothering the mind, to see beyond the blizzard of labels to this specific child, trembling and whole and real, and to this one, and then to this. And a teacher needs a heart to fully grasp the importance of that gesture, to recognize in the deepest core of your being that every child is precious, each induplicable, the one and only who will ever trod this earth, deserving of the best a teacher can give—respect, awe, reverence, commitment.

A teacher who takes up this fundamental challenge is a teacher working against the grain—you've got to have the nerve. All the pressures of schooling push teachers to act as clerks and functionaries—in terchangeable parts in a vast and gleaming and highly rationalized production line. To teach with a heart and a brain—to see education as a deeply humanizing enterprise, to teach toward opening infinite possibilities for your students—requires courage. Courage is a quality nurtured in solidarity with others—it is an achievement of people coming together freely to choose something better. In order to teach with thought and care and courage, you really need a home.

The four seekers lurching toward Oz remind us that the obstacles to our fullness as teachers will change as we develop, that there will always be more to know, always more to become, and that in our quest we must reach out for allies and friends to give us strength and power and courage to move on. And we can now know in advance that there is no wizard at the end of the road, no higher power with a magic wand to solve our all-too-human-problems. Recognizing that the people with the problems are also the people with the solutions, and that waiting for the law-makers, the system, or the union to "get it right" before we get it right is to wait a lifetime. We can look inside ourselves, then, summon strengths we never knew we had, connect up with other seekers—teachers and parents and kids—to create the schools and classrooms we deserve—thoughtful places of decency, sites of peace and freedom and justice. We are on the way, then, to our own real Emerald Cities.

We know that teaching is intellectual and ethical work. Good teachers find ways to stay alert—wide-awake—to the lives of their students. "Kidwatching" is a learnable skill that begins with a disposition of mind, an attitude, an unshakable belief that every child is a full human being, complex and dynamic, a three-dimensional creature with a heart, a spirit, an active, meaning-making mind, with hopes and aspirations that must be taken into account. Good teachers honor their students and spend some key energy figuring out how they think, experience, and make sense of the world. Good teachers, then, become students of their students in order to create more vital opportunities for real learning.

A central challenge is to see children whole, and then to create classrooms in which the visibility of persons is a common place. This is never easy; it is made excruciatingly difficult in schools where the toxic habit of labeling kids, of summing them up on the basis of a single quality or a narrow band of demonstrable skills, fragments them, constrains the visual field, and renders them opaque. An antidote to this dismal state of affairs is *kidwatching*, a faith in the proposition that all human beings have skills and capacity and experiences worthy of our attention, and the ability to observe with patience and discipline in order to intervene appropriately and with confidence. Kidwatching requires an unblinking attention to and a passionate regard for children. It means looking beyond deficit to capacity, and beyond the classroom to the world our students inhabit. The genuine and often informal out-of-school curriculum can be a source of deep understanding for what might make classroom learning take root and come alive. Children and youth are embedded in families, after all, in neighborhoods, cultural surrounds, language communities, an historic flow, an economic condition, an entire world. Kidwatchers need to bring that world into focus—a world in some important ways out of balance, in need of repair—as it smothers and challenges and shapes and touches the child.

Learning to kidwatch is an antidote, as well, to the pervasive feeling of powerlessness teachers sometimes experience in schools. No one can entirely control how you see your children—we may be manipulated, constrained, and oppressed in some aspects of our work, but we are free to awaken our minds and our hearts based on our own deepest beliefs about teaching and our own highest hopes for our students. We are freer than we sometimes know to create and enhance the environments we inhabit in order to embody our values and our dreams for our children. We can, in our journey into teaching, reach out to children and families, reach out, as well, to our colleagues as allies to create a life-long project of reverence, awe, and humility

toward our students, and with respect, too, for the enormous, transformative power of good teaching.

To teach is to choose a life of challenge.

Another challenge is to look deeply into the contexts within which
teaching occurs—social surround, historical flow, cultural web. While
the unexamined teaching life is hardly worth living, the examined life
will include pain and difficulty—after all, the contexts of our lives
include unearned privileges and undeserved suffering, murderous
drugs and deadening work, a howling sense of hopelessness for some
and the palpable threat of annihilation for others. To be aware of the
social and moral universe we inhabit and share, and to be aware, too,
of what has yet to be achieved in terms of human possibility, is to be
a teacher capable of hope and struggle, outrage and action.

But of course the teacher can only create a context, set a stage,
open a curtain. The teacher's task is excruciatingly complex precisely
because it is idiosyncratic and improvisational—as inexact as a person's
mind or a human heart, as unique and inventive as a friendship or a
love affair. The teacher's work is all about background, environment,
setting, surrounding, position, situation, connection. And relationship. Teaching is tougher than learning because teaching requires the
teacher to let others learn. Learning requires action, choice, and assent
from the student. But teaching is always undertaken without guarantees. Teaching is an act of faith.

Another basic challenge for teachers is to create an environment
that will challenge and nurture the wide range of students who will
actually appear in your classrooms. There need to be multiple entry
points toward learning and a range of routes to success. The teacher
builds the context—her or his ideas, preferences, values, instincts, and
experiences are worked up in the learning environment. It is essential
to reflect about what you value, your expectations and standards—
remember, the dimensions you are working with are not just feet and
inches but also hopes and dreams. Think about what one senses walking through the door—What is the atmosphere? What quality of experience is anticipated? What technique is dominant? What voice will be
apparent?

The intellectual work of teachers—to see students as people with
hopes, dreams, aspirations, skills, and capacities; with bodies and

minds and hearts and spirits; with experiences, histories, a past, a pathway, a future; embedded in families, neighborhoods, cultural surrounds, and language communities—is knotty and complicated, and it requires patience, curiosity, wonder, humility. It demands sustained focus, intelligent judgment, inquiry and investigation. It requires wideawakeness, since every judgment is contingent, every view partial, every conclusion tentative. The student is dynamic, alive, in motion. Nothing is settled, once and for all. No summary can be entirely authoritative. The student grows and changes—yesterday's need is forgotten, today's claims are all-encompassing and brand new. This, then, is an intellectual task of serious, massive proportion.

It also involves an ethical stance, an implied moral contract. The good teacher offers unblinking attention, even awe, and communicates a deep regard for students' lives, a respect for vulnerability. An engaged teacher begins with a belief that each student is unique, each worthy of a certain reverence. Regard extends, importantly, to an insistence that students have access to the tools with which to negotiate and perhaps even to transform the world. Love for students just as they are—without any drive or advance toward a future—is false love, enervating and disabling. The teacher must try, in good faith, to do no harm, and convince students to reach out, to reinvent, to seize an education fit for the fullest lives they might hope for.

Further, if we are to discover and develop our own relationship to the good and the just, we must understand our lives and our work as a journey or a quest. If we are to become more than clerks or robots or functionaries we must be reaching for the good, trying to repair the harm. We must see ourselves, then, as seekers, students, aspirants.

We teachers, then, need to see ourselves as in transition, in motion, works in progress. We become students of our students, in part to understand them, in part to know ourselves. A powerful reason to teach has always been to learn ourselves. Paulo Freire (1985) describes this beautifully: "Through dialogue the teacher-of-the-students and the students-of-the-teacher cease to exist and a new term emerges: teacher-student and students-teachers. The teacher is no longer merely the-one-who-teaches, but one who is himself taught in dialogue with the students, who in turn while being taught also teach. They become jointly responsible for a process in which all grow" (p. 67).

In a democracy there must be discussion, deliberation, dialogue. And while in every dialogue there are mistakes, misperceptions, struggle, and emotion, it is the disequilibrium of dialogue that leads to exploration, discovery, and change. Dialogue is improvisational and unrehearsed, and is undertaken with the serious intention of engaging others. This means we speak with the possibility of being heard, and listen with the possibility of being changed. Our conviction, then, is tempered with agnosticism and a sense of the contingent. We commit to questioning, exploring, inquiring, paying attention, going deeper. But it is not enough to put ourselves forward and assert our perspective; we must also allow for the possibility of being ourselves transformed. All of this is based on an unshakable faith in human beings. If we already know everything, we are terrible students and bad teachers. All knowledge is contingent, all inquiry limited, no perspective every perspective. To some this is cause for despair, but for teachers it might provoke some sense of trembling excitement.

With eyes wide open and riveted on learners, a further challenge to honest and righteous teachers is to stay wide-awake to the world, to the concentric circles of context in which we live and work. Teachers must know and care about some aspect of our shared life—our calling after all, is to shepherd and enable the callings of others. Teachers, then, invite students to become somehow more capable, more thoughtful and powerful in their choices, more engaged in a culture and civilization, able to participate, to embrace, and, yes, to change all that is before them. How do we warrant that invitation? How do we understand this society, this culture?

Teachers must always choose—they must choose how to see the students before them, and how to see the world as well, what to embrace and what to reject, whether to support or resist this or that directive. In schools where the insistent illusion that everything has already been settled is heavily promoted, teachers experience a constricted sense of choice, diminished imaginative space, a feeling of powerlessness regarding the basic questions of teaching and the larger purposes of education. But in these places, too, teachers must find ways to resist, to choose for the children, for the future. It is only as teachers choose that the ethical emerges. James Baldwin (1988) says:

> The paradox of education is precisely this—that as one begins to become conscious one begins to examine the society in which he is being educated. The purpose of education, finally, is to create in a person the ability to look at the world for himself, to make his own decisions, to say to himself this is black or this is white, to decide for himself whether there is a God in heaven or not. To ask questions of the universe, and then learn to live with those questions, is the way he achieves his own identity. But no society is really anxious to have that kind of person around. What societies really, ideally, want is a citizenry which will simply obey the rules of society. If a society succeeds in this, that society is about to

perish. The obligation of anyone who thinks of himself as responsible is to examine society and try to change it and to fight it—at no matter what risk. This is the only hope society has. This is the only way societies change.

We assume, then, a deep capacity in students, an intelligence (sometimes obscure, sometimes buried) as well as a wide range of hopes, dreams, and aspirations; we acknowledge, as well, obstacles to understand and overcome, deficiencies to repair, injustices to correct. With this as a base, the teacher may create an environment with abundant opportunities to practice freedom and to embody justice; to display, foster, expect, demand, nurture, allow, model, and enact inquiry toward moral action. A classroom organized in this way follows a particular rhythm: Questions focus on issues or problems (What do we need or want to know? Why is it important? How will we find out?) and on action (Given what we know now, what are we going to do about it?).

Hannah Arendt reminds us that education is where we determine whether we love the world enough to take full responsibility for it, and simultaneously whether we love our children enough to provide them entry into a given world, as well as the tools to re-energize and transform it.

Education, clearly, is political in the best sense. Schools are necessarily a conversation unfinished.

In a time when the universe of social discourse is receding and disappearing, teachers need to wonder how to continue to speak the unhearable. How can the unspoken be heard? How does self-censorship perpetuate the silence? The tension between aspiration and possibility is acute, and the question of what is to be done a daily challenge.

It is important in our work that we tell no lies and claim no easy victories. There is no easy solution, no one right way to mobilize for a better way. We must remain skeptics and agnostics, even as we stir ourselves to act on behalf of what the known demands of us. We can, then, resist becoming credulous in the face of official, authoritative knowledge, and resist as well the debilitating tendency toward cynicism about the possibility of people to act and change their lives.

Learning to teach takes time, energy, hard work. Learning to teach well requires even more: a serious and sustained engagement with the enterprise, an intense focus on the lives of children, a passionate regard for the future—that is, for the community our students will inherit and reinvent—and for the world they are arching toward.

Becoming a wonderful teacher, or a great or awesome teacher, is a lifetime affair. This is because good teaching is forever pursuing better teaching; it is always dynamic and in motion, always growing, learning, developing, searching for a better way. Teaching is never finished, never still, never easily summed up. "Wonderful Teacher" might be inscribed on someone's lifetime achievement award, printed on a retirement party banner, or etched on a tombstone, but it is never right for a working teacher. As long as I live I am under construction, becoming a teacher, learning to teach, practicing the art and craft of teaching. I'm still trying to achieve wonderfulness. Good teachers, then, are what they are not yet, and so their first and firmest rule is to reach.

Anything worth knowing or doing is a bit like this. Building friendships or a marriage or a love affair, reading novels or poems, having sex and raising children—in each of these we start off clumsy and inexperienced; with practice and reflection we can grow into wiser and more graceful participants; and as good as we might get, growth and development are still possible. Understanding life—and teaching—as infinite quest and adventure can be welcome and even heartening news. It nudges teachers to develop open and curious dispositions of mind, receptive and forgiving hearts, a stance of authentic engagement.

Teaching as an ethical enterprise goes beyond presenting what already is; it is teaching toward what ought to be. It is walking with the mothers of children, carrying the sound of the sea, exploring the outer dimensions of love. It is more than moral structures and guidelines; it includes an exposure to and understanding of material realities—advantages and disadvantages, privileges and oppressions—as well. Teaching of this kind might stir people to come together as vivid, thoughtful, and sometimes outraged. Students and teachers, then, might find themselves dissatisfied with what, only yesterday, had seemed the natural order of things. At this point, when consciousness links to conduct and upheaval is in the air, teaching becomes a call to freedom.

The fundamental message of the teacher is this: You must change your life. Whoever you are, wherever you've been, whatever you've done, the teacher invites you to a second chance, another round, perhaps a different conclusion. The teacher posits possibility, openness, and alternative; the teacher points to what could be, but is not yet. The teacher beckons you to change your path.

To teach consciously for justice and ethical action is teaching that arouses students, engages them in a quest to identify obstacles to their full humanity and the life chances of others, to their freedom, and then to drive and to move against those obstacles. And so the fundamental message of the teacher for ethical action is: You can change the world.

FURTHER READINGS

Ayers, W., & Ford, P. (1996). *City kids, city teachers: Reports from the front row*. New York: New Press.

Ayers, W., Hunt, J. A., & Quinn, T. (Eds.). (1998). *Teaching for social justice: A democracy and education reader*. New York: New Press.

Ayers, W. (1997). *A kind and just parent: The children of the juvenile court*. Boston: Beacon Press.

Bell, D. (1992). *Faces at the bottom of the well: The permanence of racism*. New York: Basic Books.

Blake, B. (1997). *She say, he say: Urban girls write their lives*. New York: State University of New York Press.

Canada, G. (1995). *Fist, stick, knife, gun: A personal history of violence in America*. Boston: Beacon Press.

Carger, C. (1996). *Of borders and dreams: A Mexican-American experience of urban education*. New York: Teachers College Press.

Deavere-Smith, A. (1997). *Fires in the mirror: Crown Heights, Brooklyn and other identities*. New York: Dramatists Play Service.

Delpit, L. (1995). *Other people's children: Cultural conflict in the classroom*. New York: New Press.

Foster, M. (1997). *Black teachers on teaching*. New York: The New Press.

Freire, P. (1985). *Pedagogy of the oppressed*. New York: Continuum.

Greene, M. (1988). *The dialectic of freedom*. New York: Teachers College Press.

Greene, M. (1995). *Releasing the imagination*. San Francisco: Jossey-Bass.

Haberman, M. (1995). *Star teachers of children of poverty*. West Lafayette, IN: Kappa Delta Pi.

Heller, C. (1997). *Until we are strong together: Women writers in the Tenderloin*. New York: Teachers College Press.

hooks, b. (1994). *Teaching to transgress: Education as the practice of freedom*. New York: Routledge.

Jelloun, B. (1999). *Racism explained to my daughter*. New York: New Press.

Kaysen, S. (1993). *Girl, interrupted*. New York: Turtle Bay Books.

Kohl, H. (1994). *"I won't learn from you": And other thoughts on creative maladjustment*. New York: New Press.

Kozol, J. (1991). *Savage inequalities: Children in American schools*. New York: Crown Pub.

Ladson-Billings, G. (1994). *The dreamkeepers: Successful teachers of African American students*. San Francisco: Jossey-Bass.

MacDonald, M. (1999). *All souls: A family story from Southie*. Boston: Beacon Press.

Malouf, D. (1993). *Remembering Babylon*. New York: Pantheon Books.

Meier, D. (1996). *The power of their ideas: A lesson for America from a small school in Harlem*. Boston: Beacon Press.

Michie, G. (1999). *Holler if you hear me: The education of a teacher and his students*. New York: Teachers College Press.

Nieto, S. (1996). *Affirming diversity: The sociopolitical context of multiracial education*. White Plains, NY: Longman.

Oe, K. (1996). *Nip the buds, shoot the kids*. New York: Grove Press.

Oyler, C. (1996). *Making room for students: Sharing teacher authority in room 104*. New York: Teachers College Press.

Perry, T. (1996). *Teaching Malcolm X*. New York: Routledge.

Peshkin, A. (1986). *God's choice: The total world of a fundamentalist Christian school*. Chicago: University of Chicago Press.

Postman, N. (1982). *The disappearance of childhood*. New York: Delacorte Press.

Rathbone, C. (1998). *On the outside looking in: A year in an inner-city high school*. New York: Atlantic Monthly Press.

Rodriguez, L. (1994). *Always running: La vida loca, gang days in L.A.* New York: Simon and Schuster.

Rose, M. (1995). *Possible lives: The promise of education in America*. Boston: Houghton Mifflin.

Silin, J. (1995). *Sex, death, and the education of children: Our passion for ignorance in the age of AIDS*. New York: Teachers College Press.

Spring, J. (1994). *Deculturalization and the struggle for equality: A brief history of the education of dominated cultures in the United States*. New York: McGraw-Hill.

Tompkins, J. (1996). *A life in school: What the teacher learned*. Reading, MA: Pursues Books.

Willis, P. (1977). *Learning to labor: How working class kids get working class jobs*. New York: Columbia University Press.

REFERENCES

Ayers, W. (1989). We who believe in freedom cannot rest until it's done. *Harvard Education Review*, 59(4), 520–528.

Baldwin, J. (1988). A talk to teachers. In R. Simonson and S. Walker, *Multicultural literacy: Opening the American mind* (pp. 3–12). St. Paul, MN: Graywolf Press.

Carini, P. F. (1979). *The art of seeing and the visibility of the person.* Grand Forks: University of North Dakota Press.

Carrol, D., & Carini, P. (1989). Assessment rooted in classroom practice: A staff review of Sid. *Insights*, 6(1), 3–8.

Delpit, L. D. (1986). Skills and other dilemmas of a progressive Black educator. *Harvard Educational Review*, 56(4), 379–385.

Delpit, L. D. (1988). The silenced dialogue: Power and pedagogy in educating other people's children. *Harvard Educational Review*, 58(3), 280–298.

Dewey, J (1938). *Experience and education.* New York: Macmillan.

Duckworth, E. (1987). *The having of wonderful ideas.* New York: Teachers College Press.

Freire, P. (1985). *Pedagogy of the oppressed.* New York: Continuum.

Gellhorn, M. (1998). "Suffer the children . . . ." In *The Library of America, Reporting Vietnam, Part one.* (pp. 287–297). New York: Author.

Greene, M. (1973). *Teacher as stranger.* Belmont, CA: Wadsworth.

Holt, J. (1990). *A life worth living: Selected letters of John Holt.* In S. Sheffer (Ed.). Columbus: Ohio State University Press.

Hubbell, S. (1988, May). The sweet bees. *The New Yorker*, pp. 45–76.

Illinois State Board of Education. (1986). *Illinois outcome statements and model learning objectives for social sciences.* Springfield, IL: Author.

Illinois State Board of Education. (1986). *State goals for learning and sample learning objectives for language arts.* Springfield, IL: Author.

Jackson, C. (1966). I don't mind. In Richard Lewis (Ed.), *Miracles* (p. 38). New York: Simon and Schuster.

Jordan, J. (1988). Nobody mean more to me than you and the future life of Willie Jordan. *Harvard Educational Review*, 58(3), 363–374.

La Escuela Fratney. (1991). *Year three.* Milwaukee: Author.

145

Lake, R. (Medicine Grizzlybear). (1990). An Indian father's plea. *Teacher Magazine, 2*(1), 48–53.

Noddings, N. (1986). Fidelity in teaching, teacher education, and research for teaching. *Harvard Educational Review, 56*(4), 496–510.

Rilke, R. M. (1934). *Letters to a young poet.* New York: Norton.

Sapon-Shevin, M. (1990). Schools as communities of love and caring. *Holistic Education Review, 3*(2), 22–24.

Schubert, W. H. (1986). *Curriculum: Paradigm, perspectives, possibilities.* New York: Macmillan.

Stanislavsky, K. (1936). *An actor prepares.* London: Routledge and Kegan Paul.

Stembridge, J. (1971). Notes about a class. In Stokely Carmichael, *Stokely speaks: Black power back to Pan-Africanism* (pp. 3–8). New York: Vintage.

Zimiles, H. (1987). Progressive education: On the limits of evaluation and the development of empowerment. *Teachers College Record, 89*(2), 203–217.

INDEX

ABOUT THE AUTHOR

William Ayers began teaching in 1965 in an experimental free school associated with the civil rights movement. He has been involved in community and adult education, prison education, and a variety of school reform projects and movements. He has taught preschool through graduate school, has lived in a residential home for "delinquent" youngsters, and has founded and directed three different alternative schools. His own children, now twenty-three, twenty, and nineteen, have been a major source for thinking and rethinking issues of teaching and learning. He is author of *The Good Preschool Teacher* (Teachers College Press, 1989), and *A Kind and Just Parent: The Children of Juvenile Court* (Beacon Press, 1997). Currently director of the Center for Youth and Society, co-director of the Small Schools Workshop, and Distinguished Professor in the College of Education at the University of Illinois at Chicago, he lives with Bernardine Dohrn, Dorothy Dohrn, his mother in law, and her companion, Florence Garcia, in Hyde Park, Chicago.